MW00775200

the real life of a

Christian Wife

100 devotions & prayers for wives

Mandy Fender

Stouthearted Publishing

Dedication

To my husband, who I love dearly . . . Thank you for all that you do for us!

&

To my mom, who taught me how to be a godly wife. Mom, I love you. Thank you for being an example!

Essentials for the Christian Wife

The Word (2 Timothy 3:16)

The Spirit (Acts 1:8)

The Fruits of the Spirit (Galatians 5:22-23)

Prayer (Matthew 6:6)

Praise (Psalm 150:1)

Worship (John 4:24)

"There is no more lovely, friendly and charming relationship, communion or company than a good marriage."

-Martin Luther

Introduction

Your marriage is beautiful . . . sometimes you just have to look past the weeds.

Whether your marriage is new and fresh or seasoned and mature, these devotions and prayers are for you—whether your marriage has no trouble at all or is in trouble, these devotions and prayers are for you! Marriage takes two, but progress in your marriage can start with you if you want it to, because God can use the wife mightily within the marital relationship. Instead of believing everything I heard about what it meant to be a Christian wife, I wanted to go straight to the Word. I did not want it to be about gender roles or what man said. I wanted to know what God said, because He is our ultimate authority.

What I have personally learned from my own marriage:

I was asked to write a paragraph of advice on marriage for one of my friends, who was soon to be married, and what I wrote kind of surprised me. I married my husband when I was very young—seventeen, to be exact—and at the time of writing this, I had been married fourteen years. I know marriage is wonderful and beautiful, and all sorts of lovely, but I also know the hard truth of making a marriage what it should be. Here is what I wrote to my friend:

Congratulations, I am so excited for you! If I could tell you anything about marriage, I would tell you marriage is commitment, sacrifice, and work . . . and most importantly, a covenant. I know that not all of those words sound fun to most as they are not all warm and fuzzy, butterflies-in-your-stomach type of words, but they are the truth and anyone married over ten years will say the same. Don't get me wrong, marriage is also beautiful and full of love, laughter, and getting to spend your entire life with your best friend. Adventures full of joy and expectation will undoubtedly take place; so will hardships. The important thing is that husband and wife walk through both together. That's what makes a marriage strong. That's what will make your marriage stand the test of time. When the laughter falls flat, and words fail, remember what marriage is—commitment, sacrifice, work, and most importantly, a covenant. It's God, you, and your spouse against the world. Now, go take the world by storm!

Marriage is not always sunshine and rainbows, and sometimes it can be a downright challenge/struggle (however you'd like to say it) to be a godly wife. While I was in New Mexico, God showed me something extraordinary about my marriage. I was standing in the middle of a gorgeous, scenic mountain range and in front of the snow-capped mountains were weeds that had grown over knee-high. You see, the backdrop was stunning, even the sky displayed beautiful colors that only God could create, and right there, He showed me that behind the weeds of marriage that may have grown over time, there is still beauty. I just have to look for it.

The truth is marriage is hard sometimes. It's not always easy. Not everything in marriage is romantic or movie worthy, yet marriage is indeed beautiful and one of the most important decisions you have ever made in your life. I wanted to write this book to encourage fellow Christian wives and let them know that they are not alone in this journey of figuring out who they are and where they stand in marriage. My hope is to give you the Word of God and not my opinion.

I don't want to be bound by archaic traditions that we hold on to simply because it's what has always been done, but rather, know the truth of who I am as a wife in the Word of God. We live in the twenty-first century and have all these expectations thrown in our faces and old-school opinions from elders, as well as new-age culture trying to shape our marriages and the way we think marriage should be, but there is no way we can please everyone. We need to know what God has said, not what man has said.

As I write this book, I want you to know that it is just as much for me as it is for you. I hope to grow right along with you as you read this. I am still learning what being a godly wife means, but if you're reading this, please know, you are a part of my tribe—the tribe of Christian women doing their best to be godly wives. I am in the trenches with you, my sister, and I hope you are encouraged as you read each devotion and prayer.

I am praying for the marriages of every woman who holds this book in her hands. I may not know you by name, but I know that God sees both of us and He will work in our marriages in Jesus's name!

The ultimate question I want to answer for myself and other wives is:

Who has God called *us* to be to *our own husbands*?

The only thing that stands when all else fails is the Word of God and that's what we, as wives, should continually look to so that we may know this answer for ourselves. Each individual is unique; therefore, each marriage is unique as well, but God has given instruction that will pertain to each marriage and will fill the gaps and answer the questions we have concerning marriage. What's right? What's wrong? What matters? What doesn't? I know the Bible has the answers! I cannot tell you how many times the Word of God has strengthened my marriage when nothing else could. There is hope for your marriage and for you as a wife! And even if your marriage is great, it is always good to have Biblical reminders of who you are in Christ!

What I want you to know before reading:

I want you to know that I understand that, in marriage, not everything falls upon the wife. I know that the responsibility of a relationship takes two and that each individual must give effort, but since this is a book to help women become better wives, I do focus mainly on their growth and knowledge of the Word. Husbands have assignments too, but I want to focus on our assignment as wives. I hope you hear my heart and know that I understand that concept completely—husbands are responsible for their actions too. Now, you do what you can do!

For the wives with Christian husbands:

Praise God your husband believes and is most likely doing his best to be a godly husband to you as well. I know that Christian husbands are not without their own faults and struggles. I know this because I am married to one. We have had our loud "disagreements," the times we don't get along, and the times we are discouraged with one another. My heart is to remind you and encourage you through the good times and the bad times of marriage, God is always there. Whether you have a wonderful marriage or a marriage that seems to be falling apart, I hope these devotions give you the strength to be the type of wife God has called you to be and for the prayers to help you and your husband grow closer together and in Christ. I pray you, your husband,

and marriage are strengthened, encouraged, and blessed in Jesus's name, amen!

For the wives with husbands who don't yet believe:

I say *yet* because I believe that God can work through the wife to show the love of Christ to the husband. There is even a devotion entitled 'The Wife's Power' that shares a scripture that will bring hope to you. I may not know what it is like to be married to a man who does not believe, but I did grow up in a household where my mother had to step up and be the spiritual leader of the home. I saw my mom cry and struggle with my dad, yet never waver in her faith. She remained true to what the Word of God said a wife should be, and now, my dad has faith in God like I have never seen before, all because my mom stayed faithful to God and what He had said a wife could be to her husband. My mom was the love of Christ and showed my dad the true meaning of marriage, commitment, and sacrifice. I want you to know that there is hope for you and your marriage too! I pray for your strength and courage as a wife and I pray for your husband's salvation in Jesus's name, amen!

Now, let's get to it!

1

Relationship Goals

Song of Solomon 4:9 (ESV) "You have captivated my heart, my sister, my bride; you have captivated my heart with one glance of your eyes, with one jewel of your necklace."

Have you ever seen those cute, perfect couples in movies, or books, or television shows who seem to have no cares in the world and said, "I wish I had a relationship with my husband like that." I must admit, I have wished that a time or two, but I had to come to the realization that those so-called perfect couples were fiction and, even if they were real, like reality television (if we can call that real), they were still in front of a camera and probably on their best relationship behavior. I learned that I must set a realistic goal for my marriage, not a make-believe one. The truth is, bills still have to be paid, jobs have to be worked, dishes have to be washed, laundry folded, and children have to be fed. Not everything is going to be this big romantic gesture and that's okay. I had to learn to give my husband grace just like Jesus gives me grace on a daily basis. I love my husband and, no, we are not perfect, but we have reached my hashtag status of relationship goals. I can totally see us old on the front porch in rocking chairs still holding hands and looking into each other's eyes. And who said the romance factor should only fall on the husband? Wives can do something romantic for their husbands too. Is there anything that you know your hubby would love? Maybe surprise him and spark the romance alive again. Have you set any unrealistic relationship goals? Break them. Appreciate what you have and cultivate it to see it grow. No, your marriage may not look like the ones in the movies, but that's okay. Real life and real marriage are more beautiful anyway. Captivate his heart!

Prayer:

Lord, open my eyes to see the beauty of my own marriage. Help me to appreciate my relationship where it's at and show me how I can nourish it to see it grow. In Jesus's name, amen.

2

The Truth about Submission

Ephesians 5:22 (ESV) "Wives, submit to your own husbands, as to the Lord."

In the climate in which we live, the word "submission" has gotten this negative connotation attached to it, as if it was a dirty, degrading word when, in fact, it is a word that actually signifies an intense commitment to one another. "Submission" is not a curse word. In my understanding, submission is a conscious choice by the wife to submit to her husband, which takes wisdom and humility, and which, ultimately, is a sign of a strong woman, not a weak one. While we, as the wife, are to submit to our own husband, a husband is to love his wife and give himself up for her as Christ did for the church (Ephesians 5:25). The husband actually has a requirement set upon Him as well. I do not believe God was putting His thumb on women, keeping them down when requiring this of wives, but rather protecting, loving, and giving the godly task of submission to the woman, who He knew would be able to do so because He created us, after all, and knows what we can handle. Biblical submission is not about one controlling another or dominating the other; Biblical submission is one loving another in a way that requires trust in God, compassion, and faith. The truth of submission is that it takes someone who knows who they are in Christ, a godly woman, to submit. As you submit to your husband, remember that you first must submit to Christ and He will guide you to what the truth of submission to your husband really is by His standards. Remember, Biblical submission is not demeaning or degrading, but a sign of a strong woman who trusts God, not man.

Prayer:

Lord, as I submit to You, teach me how to godly submit to my husband. Allow my heart to open up to Your truth and open my eyes to love as You would have me to love my husband. Give me the courage to submit to my own husband the way You see fit. In Jesus's name, amen.

3

Building the Home

Proverbs 14:1 (ESV) "The wisest of women builds her house . . ."

My husband said something once, and I have never forgotten it to this day. He said, "I may pay for this house, *but you*, you make it a home." Yeah, I just about melted when he said it. Whether your husband has said this or not, the truth is, as the wife, you set the tone/atmosphere of your home. I guess that is where the saying "happy wife, happy life" came from. There is just something about the dynamic of being a wife which allows you to build up your spouse, or tear him down. There is a reason your husband chose you out of all the women out there. Most godly men understand that their wife's well-being is important and makes the difference within the home. On the home front, the wife stands on the frontlines for her marriage and family. Remember that as you go about your day-to-day schedule. Keep your home a priority because it matters. Both wife and husband have a responsibility to make the home a safe place for one another. Only you can control what you do for the home, so do what you can where you can and build your home!

Prayer:

Lord, I ask for Your help and guidance as I build my home and I know I must build my home in You for it to stand. Let the foundation for my marriage be the same foundation my salvation is built on, which is your Son, Jesus Christ. In Jesus's name, amen.

4

Communication is Key

James 1:19 (ESV) "Know this, my beloved brothers: let every person be quick to hear, slow to speak, slow to anger."

Most of the time, women are great communicators, but sometimes, in marriage, we don't always say what we mean. Men often refer to this as "speaking in code," and they have no idea what their wives are really saying. For instance, "everything's fine" does not necessarily translate to everything really being fine. The internal dialogue women can have with themselves can be quite confusing for their spouses. The key for wives (and husbands) is to listen to hear and not only to reply. Try to listen to your husband and hear him out, and then after thoughtful consideration, speak from the heart. Your husband can't read your mind, so learn to communicate with him in a way that works for the both of you. Not saying what you mean has a way of getting misunderstood and then opens the door for resentment. Ask God to help you daily to communicate with your husband in a way that he will respond to and understand. Remember, nagging and voicing an opinion is not the same thing. Speak with love and use a Holy Ghost filter when you listen and when you speak.

Prayer:

Lord, help me to guard my tongue and not hurt my husband with my words. Let my words be what You want me to say and how You want me to say them. I pray I truly hear my husband's heart and he hears mine. In Jesus's name, amen.

5

Hard Work Pays Off

2 John 1:8 (ESV) "Watch yourselves, so that you may not lose what we have worked for, but may win a full reward."

This verse is referring to watching out for deceivers and holding fast to the truth of salvation, but I also believe it can be applied to marriage. You must guard your marriage and put in the work to sustain it. The longevity of a marriage is the responsibility of both the husband and the wife. The work you put in will produce the result you will see. Anyone who says marriage is easy has probably never been married, or has only been married for a short period of time, because marriage is, at times, work, and sometimes, very hard work. Invest in your relationship with your husband because the dividends are worth the challenge. I understand there may be words exchanged and disagreements, but if you place your marriage in the hands of God, then also put in the work God asks you to for your marriage, to not just survive, but thrive. Your marriage does not have to just be another number on a statistic board. Your marriage can defy the charts when you put in the effort and give God the relationship. As you grow closer to Christ, allow Him to strengthen the bond with your spouse. Pray for your husband and praise God for him. Put in the work to protect, nurture, and grow your marriage and it will pay off.

Prayer:

Lord, let me grow closer to my spouse and help me to do my part in the relationship so that I may not lose what I have worked hard for but hold on to the treasure that is marriage and my relationship with my husband. In Jesus's name, amen.

6

A Wife's Wisdom

Ephesians 5:15-16 (ESV) "Look carefully then how you walk, not as unwise but as wise, making the best use of the time, because the days are evil."

Women are notoriously known for being excellent multi-taskers. They can have a thousand "browsers" open in their minds and not miss a beat. I believe God created women as such because He knew all that being a wife/mother would entail. With such responsibility, wisdom plays a vital role in a wife's life. Whether the decisions are seemingly menial or of utmost importance, the wife has to be quick on her feet and use discernment every single day, and thus, the necessity for wisdom. In marriage, a wife's wisdom can prove to be extraordinary. Now, your husband may never ask you for your opinion, but your wisdom is still crucial and can help lead both you and your spouse to better choices concerning the present and future. The times are certainly evil and a wife's wisdom can benefit the marriage even outside of the home. Look carefully at your marriage walk and walk wisely within it, making the best use of your time as a loving, caring, and supportive wife. As a wife, your wisdom can save thousands of dollars, and help your family to live better.

Prayer:

Lord, I pray for wisdom in my life—wisdom in my
marriage, finances, future, and every task I do as a wife.
Help me to make smart choices in and for my marriage.
In Jesus's name, amen.

7

The Pursuit of Love in Marriage

1 Corinthians 14:1 (ESV) ". . . Pursue love . . ."

Never lose sight of why you loved your husband in the first place. Remember those butterflies you felt when he held your hand for the first time, or the first kiss? Don't forget what brought you and your husband together. *Love*. Love for one another, for what they stood for, for who they were as a person. Some think that after marriage there is no need to pursue, but wives should continually pursue love with their husbands and vice versa. More marriages would last if they had continually pursued love within the marriage. The grass is not greener on the other side; you may just need to water your "marriage grass" a little more. If you have ever had the feeling of falling out of love with your spouse, I challenge you to write down all of the things that made you love him in the first place, and love him all over again, like it was the first time. Say "I love you" regularly, and mean it. Let your pursuit of love in marriage shine through in the good times and, yes, in the bad times too. Love your husband and let him know that you love him. Maybe even consider doing something nice for him just because you love him. If there is love, there is always hope!

Prayer:

Lord, I want to pursue love in my marriage. Help me to express my love for my husband and to also have that love reciprocated by him so that our marriage may be one that continually pursues love. In Jesus's name, amen.

8

A Trustworthy Wife

Proverbs 31:11 (NLT) "Her husband can trust her, and she will greatly enrich his life."

As I have studied the Bible to see what a wife is to her husband, I often find that wives are great pillars of trust and security for their spouses. A husband who can trust his wife can rest assured that his home life is one that he does not have to worry about, which can lift a whole lot of stress off of him. In turn, the wife should be able to trust the husband with her life and future. Trust within a marriage should be mutual and respected. The wife is much like a lighthouse for the husband, giving him light and offering hope, even in the darkest of times. Let your husband know that he can trust you by exercising discretion and loyalty. Let him know he can depend on you to be a safe place—a place of comfort and rest. Just as a husband is to make the wife feel safe and secure, so should the wife her husband. If he speaks with you in confidence, respect that, just as you would expect him to, regarding your discussion with him. Your marriage should be a place of trust between both parties. Never run your marriage or spouse into the dirt by speaking negatively about it/him to your girlfriends. If you have a concern about your spouse, you always have a confidant in God in which you can openly talk about your marriage in complete confidence and gossip won't be a result.

Prayer:

Lord, I pray I am a trustworthy wife and that my husband knows he can trust me; likewise, help me to be able to trust my husband, and make him trustworthy within our marriage. In Jesus's name, amen.

9

You're a Good Thing!

Proverbs 18:22 (ESV) "He who finds a wife finds a good thing and obtains favor from the Lord."

I want to use this page to remind you how much you rock as a wife! You are a gift to your husband, a true blessing. Being a wife has a lot of demands and can sometimes feel a bit overwhelming. It may seem like each scripture and verse require so much more of you and very little of him, but trust me, that is not true. This book is meant for wives, hence all of the concentration on Biblical wifely duties falling on the wife, and the responsibility therein. That's simply because this book is geared toward becoming a godly wife. Please remember, you are a good thing! When you are a godly wife, your husband is so blessed to have you by his side and in his life! As a wife, you are a good thing to your husband. You are a helpmate and a partner in this thing called life. If marriage was a movie, it would be full of suspense, action, comedy, drama, romance. Every day would hold something different, but do you know what would be the same? The husband and wife would stay by each other's sides, helping one another, laughing with each other, and kicking villains' tails together through it all. You, my friend, wife to one husband, are

23

a good thing! Don't you dare forget that!

Prayer:

Lord, make me remember through all of the responsibility that I am a blessing and a good thing to my husband. Whether he sees it or acknowledges it, remind me that it is a good thing to be a godly wife. In Jesus's name, amen.

10

Stuck Like Glue

Genesis 2:24 (ESV) "Therefore, a man shall leave his father and his mother and hold fast to his wife, and they shall become one flesh."

Saying "I do" is committing to living and sharing your life with someone else, fully and completely. My husband and I got married very young and he used to say, "You and me against the world!" That was a cute way of saying he had my back and I had his. There is no greater feeling than knowing that someone is truly there for you, no matter what, and at all times. I often believe that is why God uses marriage so much to describe our relationship with Christ, because there is a bond that connects a husband and wife that nothing else can replicate, even though there are people that would try. Marriage is beautiful in the fact that together, husband and wife are stronger. Allow yourself to grow close to your husband by letting God break down walls in your life that other men may have caused you to build. Your husband is a gift to you as well, one that you decided to leave the past behind for and become one flesh with. As you allow God to be the glue that holds you together, let Him also be the glue that unites you to your husband in marriage. God first equals a better marriage. The stronger your relationship with Christ, the stronger your marriage bond can be as well.

Prayer:

Lord, tear down the walls that have been preventing me from fully enjoying life with my husband and help me to bond with him in a greater way. In Jesus's name, amen.

11

Husbands Should Not Be Harsh

Colossians 3:18-19 (ESV) "Wives, submit to your husbands, as is fitting in the Lord. Husbands, love your wives, and do not be harsh with them."

Can I just be honest and say I LOVE the second part of this verse! Of course, right? But for now, let's check out the first part. There's that word "submission" again. From what I understand, I see God placing great importance on how a husband treats his wife. He should be a leader worth following. As a man follows Christ and loves his wife as Christ loves the church, it is easier for the wife to submit because the husband is worthy of that submission by being a godly husband. It's important to know that your husband should not be harsh with you, not in actions or words, but sometimes they are and I know it hurts our hearts when they do. I also know God will help us to submit as wives and help our husbands to be leaders worth following. If your husband is harsh, I beseech you to seek God concerning your relationship. The most important thing you can do is allow God into your marriage, whether your husband is saved or not. Keep studying what godly marriage is and seek counsel should you need to. It's important you feel safe within your marriage as well. A godly husband will make mistakes and misspeak sometimes, but he will also allow the Lord to correct him concerning his treatment of you. Stay strong. God is able to see you and your marriage through!

Prayer:

Lord, I pray my marriage follows this verse as an example to help guide both of us into a greater understanding of what a godly marriage is. Work in my husband's heart to be kinder and gentler toward me and help me through any storms we may face. In Jesus's name, amen.

12

Respect

Ephesians 5:33 (ESV) "However, let each one of you love his wife as himself, and let the wife see that she respects her husband."

Within marriage, there should be a mutual respect—a respect that is loving, honest, and compassionate. Respect often begets respect. As you respect your husband, your husband will most likely show respect to you. According to the dictionary, respect is deep admiration for another. How perfect of a fit is that in marriage, for a wife and husband should admire one another. Most men have a sense of pride and in this verse God is telling husbands to love their wives as they love themselves, meaning they take pride in their wives (adore them). Take the time in your marriage to relish in all the good your husband has done and everything that you admire about him. Give him the respect that is befitting of a godly wife to her godly husband. As you sow respect into your husband, I believe you will reap respect from him as well. Marriage is a blessing where mutual respect should be given one to the other. May you and your husband both be respectful as God sees fit.

Prayer:

Lord, I pray that I would respect my husband as You would want me to respect him and for my husband to love me as he loves himself. Let us grow closer together through mutual admiration and respect. In Jesus's name, amen.

13

The Marriage Bed

1 Corinthians 7:2-5 (ESV) "But because of the temptation to sexual immorality, each man should have his own wife and each woman her own husband. The husband should give to his wife her conjugal rights, and likewise the wife to her husband. For the wife does not have authority over her own body, but the husband does. Likewise, the husband does not have authority over his own body, but the wife does. Do not deprive one another, except perhaps by agreement for a limited time, that you may devote yourselves to prayer; but then come together again, so that Satan may not tempt you because of your lack of self-control."

The only safe place to have sex is within the confines of marriage, and as such, should not be shied away from when married. Sex was designed by God and is not evil, but beautiful in marriage. Physical intimacy isn't everything in marriage, but it is a part of it. As a woman, you may not have the same drive as your husband or he may not have the same drive as you, but opening up a dialogue with him concerning intimacy will help you see where he stands, and how he feels, and an opportunity to share how you feel. Use the communication you have prayed for and be open with your spouse. It can be embarrassing, but asking God to help you meet your husband's needs, as well as your own, will certainly only benefit the intimacy between you and your husband. The marriage bed can bring about a physical and an emotional companionship, which creates a deeper bond and stronger union. Ask God to help you see the beauty and companionship gained in the marriage bed and keep an open line of communication with your husband regarding the physical love between the two of you.

Prayer:

Lord, help me to be open with my husband and work on my heart concerning sex and physical intimacy with my husband. In Jesus's name, amen.

14

A Wife's Power

1 Peter 3:1-2 (ESV) "Likewise, wives, be subject to your own husbands, so that even if some do not obey the word, they may be won without a word by the conduct of their wives, when they see your respectful and pure conduct."

A wife's conduct has the power to lead her husband to Christ—to point him in the direction of salvation through Jesus. Most women like to talk, but when words fail, a wife still has power in the way she behaves. Husbands can be won to the Lord without words! The sheer act of a wife's respectfulness and pure conduct can show a wife's husband the way, truth, and life. If your husband already knows the Lord, let your behavior be an example by which to show him and remind him of how good God truly is. As women, we have an innate skill to nurture and love that can be used to continually glorify God in our marriage. I believe that a wife's power is greater than most wives know. You can make a difference within your household and within your marriage. Think about this verse in every action you take within marriage and, as you think about it, allow God to use you so that He may work on your husband's heart through what he sees in you.

Prayer:

Lord, I ask You, today, to use me from this point
forward to show my husband Your love, grace, and
mercy. I pray my behavior is pleasing to You and will
help to strengthen my relationship with my husband,
and I declare my husband is saved and that I see the
transformation You are doing in him. In Jesus's name,
amen.

15

The Praying Wife

Matthew 6:6 (NIV) **"But when you pray, go into your room, close the door and pray to your Father, who is unseen. Then your Father, who sees what is done in secret, will reward you."**

Have you ever just not known what to do about your relationship with your husband? Or . . . Do you know your husband is really going through something and you're not sure how you can help? The answer is and always will be PRAYER. Prayer is something you can always do for your spouse whether you know what to do for him or not. Prayer tethers you to the One who has the answer and who is the answer. As you see a need within your family, take that to God through prayer. All you have to do is speak, laying out your heart for God to hear, and then listen. Listen to that still, small voice in your soul, go to the Word, and get confirmation on what you should do. This act will help you not only in marriage but in every aspect of your life as well. A praying wife is a strong wife, a praying wife is a helpful wife, a praying wife is able to stand when everything else around her seems to be falling down. Yes, dear friend, prayer will give you the strength you need in marriage. If you have not really, sincerely prayed for your marriage in a while, NOW is the time to start because prayer will make a difference! Don't worry about anything, pray about everything!

Prayer:

Lord, I come to You on behalf of my husband. I pray he knows that You are the answer and that both of us learn to lean on You and not on our own understanding. Instead of worrying about my marriage, remind me to pray about it and go to You concerning every one of my needs. In Jesus's name, amen.

16

So Much to Offer

Proverbs 31:18 (NIV) "She sees that her trading is profitable, and her lamp does not go out at night."

Christian wife, you, yes, YOU have so much to offer. Don't count yourself short. What you bring to the table for your husband and family, no one else can bring, no matter what they say. Put your hands to work within your marriage and see that your effort and what you do is profitable. Maintain the oil in your spiritual lamp and never let it go out. Your husband needs you and what you do more than he might say. Maybe you feel underappreciated or your work is undervalued, but you must see that what you do is important, because it is. Whether you solely take care of the home, raise the children, or work and help pay the bills, you offer so much and your preparedness helps the entire household. A wife often sees what a husband can't in the home and can prepare accordingly. A wife keeps everything running smoothly and efficiently. Without a wife, a husband is missing an important piece of his life, a piece of life that helps keep everything moving. You, Christian wife, have so much to offer. You are appreciated and valued. Thank you for being you! Thank you for the lunches packed and dinners made. Thank you for the trips back and forth that you make. Thank you for keeping your family going! Honestly, you deserve kudos. In my heart, I'm yelling, "Hey, someone get this Christian wife a trophy or something!" I know you don't do it for the accolades, but I just wanted to acknowledge all that you do! I know being a Christian wife is challenging and requires a lot, so I wanted to be sure you knew that there is someone out there rooting for you!

Prayer:

Lord, I pray that my husband sees and is grateful for what I bring to the table, but even if he doesn't, let me know how important my job is and that the work I do is not in vain. Lord, help me keep everything running smoothly. In Jesus's name, amen.

17

Loneliness in Marriage

Isaiah 41:10 (NIV) "So do not fear, for I am with you; do not be dismayed, for I am your God. I will strengthen you and help you; I will uphold you with my righteous right hand."

It breaks my heart to have to write this devotion because marriage is supposed to mean you never feel alone, right? But that simply is not true. Sometimes, in marriage, it's lonely; like you're stuck on a secluded island all by yourself and no one is there to help you out, no one to take you home again. Whether your husband travels a lot for work, is in the military, or even right at home in the living room, you may have the feeling of loneliness. I want you to know that I have been there. There have been times when I felt like there was no one to talk to and that my husband didn't even care (this was not true but it did not change the fact that that was how I felt). Feeling alone within marriage happens sometimes, but there is Someone who is right by your side, always. God is there with you. You are never truly alone; not in marriage, not in life, not in anything. Next time you feel completely alone, remember who is there. If you seek Him, you will find Him even in the midst of your loneliness.

Prayer:

Lord, the next time I am lonely help me to remember that You are there. I give You my loneliness and pray that You open my husband's heart to see that I need him emotionally present in my life and for him to really be there for me, even while miles away. In Jesus's name, amen.

18

The 'D' Word

Ephesians 5:31 (ESV) "Therefore a man shall leave his father and mother and hold fast to his wife, and the two shall become one flesh."

Divorce . . . No matter how bad you want to say it during an argument, this word should not be thrown around or used lightly. I know couples who use this word to escalate the exchange when fighting with their spouse, and I always tell them not to because I know out of the abundance of the heart the mouth speaks. If anyone says this word so casually and freely then there is a chance they have thought about it, or it will make them think about it, even worse, it might make the reality of it an easier possibility because they have thrown it into the atmosphere and to the other's heart. Biblical reasons for divorce are few and far between, so be careful when slinging this word around as an insult because it is a spiritual slap-in-the-face to your husband. If he throws around this word to you, you do not have to engage. Take a deep breath and evaluate your words wisely. If you see that a fight is about to escalate, ask God how you can bring it down. It's important that both you and your husband learn how to communicate with one another without going for the jugular. Maybe make an agreement with your husband that you nor he will say this word to hurt the other. Instead, learn to communicate with one another in love and compassion. Misunderstandings, disagreements, and miscommunications are inevitable when you are with someone for a longer period of time, so know that it's a normal part of marriage that does not have to get out of hand. You and your husband are like one flesh. To break apart will be painful for both of you. A good rule is to always put yourself in your spouse's shoes and see his side of things too.

Prayer:

Lord, help me to not use the word "divorce" when fighting with my husband, and if my husband says it please help me to not become bitter. Help us both to be better spouses to one another even in our disagreements. In Jesus's name, amen.

19

Going Through the Motions

Proverbs 5:18 (NIV) "May your fountain be blessed, and may you rejoice in the wife of your youth."

Has your marriage ever been stuck in a rut, like you were getting nowhere? Or . . . Have you ever felt that you were just going through the motions of marriage? Sometimes marriage can become routine or seem like you are on a hamster's wheel, just doing the same things over and over again. Going to bed just to wake up the next morning to repeat the same day. They say that there are marks of time within the marriage such as "the seven-year itch" based off an old movie where a faithful husband gets tempted because of the boredom with monogamy. If most wives were truthful, they would say they have felt like they have been "stuck" or bored with the routine of marriage at one point or another, but I want to look at how great routine and monogamy can be. You know what I feel after fourteen years of marriage to the same man? Comfortable, which is not a bad thing! My favorite pair of jeans are my favorite because they're comfortable. I can live in them, breathe in them, move in them. (Yes, I totally just compared the comfort of marriage to my comfortable jeans; it worked for me.) But, I really mean it.

Monogamy . . . marriage . . . routine brings me not only comfort but security. I may not get the butterflies like I once did, but you know what I do get? A reassurance that every day I have a husband who loves me and is willing to stay with me even in the most routine days of life and that, my friends, is beautiful. And who says you can't spice things up, go somewhere new, or try something different with your hubby? You're both grown adults; go on an adventure if you'd like! May you be blessed by the spouse of your youth!

Prayer:

Lord, even in the routine let me love my husband and open up my eyes to the beauty that is in my marriage in the everyday things. Help me to appreciate the little things and rejoice in the comfort of a solid, monogamous marriage. In Jesus's name, amen.

20

Same Team

Matthew 19:5 (KJV) "For this cause shall a man leave father and mother, and shall cleave to his wife."

Have you noticed that there is a whole lot of cleaving going on between husband and wife in the scriptures? This same verse is found in Ephesians as well and I used it for an earlier devotion, but for this one, I want to point out that you and your hubby are on the same team! Cleave means to adhere closely/loyally, stick to, or to cling. My daughter plays basketball and when her team is trying to get a rebound they get so revved up that when one of their teammates rebound the ball with them they don't notice the other hands on the ball belong to their teammate and not an opponent. I am always yelling out, "SAME TEAM . . . SAME TEAM!!!" To you and your hubby, I say the same thing, "Same team!" Examine your marriage. Are you so caught up in your life that you have forgotten that you have a teammate right beside you? This devotion, I want to remind you and encourage you that although you and your husband may have very different styles and opinions, you both are on the same team, which is your marriage. Fight for your marriage, not against your spouse, because, after all, a win for him is a win for you and vice versa.

45

Prayer:

Lord, I pray I cleave to my husband and that I remember that we are on the same team. Help me to acknowledge his victories and to rejoice with him when he rejoices. In Jesus's name, amen.

21

Guard Your Heart

Proverbs 4:23 (NIV) "Above all else, guard your heart, for everything you do flows from it."

Have you ever heard of the phrases "Oh, be careful little eyes what you see," and "Be careful little ears what you hear"? Or "Hear no evil, see no evil, speak no evil"? There is much credence to those old hymns and sayings. The Bible clearly lets us know to guard our heart. How do we do that? We do that by abstaining from appearances of evil, refusing to allow our eyes and ears to hear or be around ungodly things, or behavior. You can protect your marriage when you guard your heart. You can protect your relationship with your husband when you guard your heart. I hate to even bring this up but I have to . . . erotica, both in film and in literature, is not the way God wants you to enhance your love for your husband. That is not a godly way of "spicing things up." Be careful what you let into your mind because it will sink into your heart and distort what being a godly wife and having a godly marriage really is about. Guard your heart against worldly things that will, in the end, wind up hurting you and your spouse.

Prayer:

Lord, guard my heart and give me the courage to
abstain from anything that would hinder my
relationship with my husband, and I pray my husband
guards his heart and give him the strength to do right by
You and our marriage. In Jesus's name, amen.

22

A Soft Answer

Proverbs 15:1 (ESV) "A soft answer turns away wrath, but a harsh word stirs up anger."

In the heat of the moment, I know how hard it is to reply to your husband with a soft answer, but I have found out that a soft answer does indeed turn away wrath. It's important to understand that giving a soft answer does not mean you are soft. Giving a soft answer means you have learned to do what the Bible has said and that is a sign of wisdom, not softness. Do you want to have a winning marriage? Then learn how to give a soft answer. Most men hate to be nagged, but a soft answer, on the other hand, will open them up to listen rather than combat what you have just said. You will always, ALWAYS, catch more flies with honey than with vinegar. As a wife, you must ask yourself . . . Do I really want to stir up anger by raising my voice just as loud or even louder than his to get my point across, or do I want to apply the Word of God and turn away wrath? Women of God, battles are not won in marriage by your savvy alone, you need the Word! I challenge you to prove this scripture in your life, and the next time you want to speak harshly, think before you speak and give a soft answer and see how your husband responds. Who knows, you may very well just blow his mind by the way you reply/respond!

Prayer:

Lord, my prayer is that I learn how to respond with a soft answer. Give me the words to speak and teach me how to say them. In Jesus's name, amen.

23

Check Your Attitude

Proverbs 27:15 (NLT) "A quarrelsome wife is as annoying as constant dripping on a rainy day."

Ouch. That's about as plain as the Word can say it. If you are quarrelsome, you're annoying. Hey, I did not say it, the WORD did. Think about a rain storm. Now, think about being in your nice, cozy home, but wait, there's a hole in the roof, and the rain that would normally be relaxing is dripping all over your carpet. Drip . . . drip . . . drip . . . drip . . . Not fun, right? Most likely, all you can focus on is that stinkin' leak that just won't stop and it's ruining your home, stealing away time and rest. That's probably how your husband feels if you quarrel with him all the time. Do you really want your husband to feel that way? Do you really want to be the annoying wife? I know I don't want to be. There's a difference between asking your husband, telling your husband, and nagging your husband. I learned that when I ask my husband in a kind way, I get a much better turnout than when I tell my husband to do something. I know every relationship is dynamic and that your husband may be okay with you telling him what to do, but if he isn't . . . don't. He's not a child, even if he acts like one, and you're not his mother. And yes, that may mean you have to just do it yourself, which is frustrating too, I know, but with God, it is possible to learn your spouse. So where is the line drawn between asking, telling, and nagging and being quarrelsome? No one knows your husband's personality and triggers better than you, so learn what works and what doesn't. Be pleasant and realistic. If the "honey do" list is bothersome to your husband, find another way to present it. The key is attitude, attitude, attitude. Keep a cool head and a calm attitude and you and your husband will end up enjoying life a lot more.

Prayer:

Lord, right now search my heart and attitude. Allow me to see when I am losing my cool and help me to adjust my attitude toward my husband accordingly. If I am like a constant dripping to my husband, I pray for Your guidance to not be so anymore. And help me to learn to say "I'm sorry" to my husband when I need to. In Jesus's name, amen.

24

The Joyful Wife

Habakkuk 3:18 (NIV) ". . . yet I will rejoice in the LORD, I will be joyful in God my Savior."

In this passage of scripture, Habakkuk found himself in a hard place, saying that should the fig tree not blossom, and should no fruit come, and should the flock be cut off, his joy was still found in the Lord. It's important to know and understand that ultimately your joy does not come from your husband, but from your Father, God. Marriage is always going to be a process of growth, and sometimes your husband will make you happy and sometimes he won't, but God is your true source of joy, and the joy He gives will sustain you. If you can learn to find joy in God at the big events of life, like weddings, births, and vacations, *and* the little everyday tasks of the mundane, like staying home, eating at the table, and driving somewhere together, then you will soon realize what joy really is. Joy is not an event or a place. It is a state of being where the soul is that can't be stolen by circumstance because circumstance did not give it and cannot, therefore, take it away. In marriage, remember where your joy comes from.

Prayer:

Lord, give me the joy that only You can give and let me be a joyful wife who cherishes every moment with her husband. Remind me that my joy is found in You! In Jesus's name, amen.

25

Taking the Time to Care

1 Corinthians 10:12 (KJV) "Wherefore let him that thinketh he standeth take heed lest he fall."

This passage is referring to our relationship with the Lord and gives caution to pay attention and be careful so that we do not fall. Our very first priority as Christian wives is our relationship with Jesus Christ. If we are not secure in Him, how can we ever be secure in our marriage? For this devotion, take the time to care about your heavenly relationship so that your earthly relationships can be strengthened. As you mature in Christ, you will mature as a Christian wife. After you tend to your relationship with God, take the time to really care about your relationship with your husband. Let him know that you see him, *really see him,* and all that he does for the family. Care about his well-being and what he has to say. I know I have a tendency to zone out a little bit, so I am making a conscious effort to care and show that I care to my husband. It's time to start caring for yourself too. A lot of women put themselves on the backburner, so to speak, and I am not so sure that is a healthy way to live either. Take the time to care about your relationship with God, your relationship with your husband, and take care of yourself physically, mentally, and spiritually. Ultimately, take heed of every aspect of your life and tend to it. It's important. You're important. Take the time to care. The effort you put in will be the results that you see.

Prayer:

Lord, I pray that I learn to care more about my relationship with You and my husband, and that I take the time to care for myself as well. Help me to take the time to care. In Jesus's name, amen.

26

A Forgiving Wife

2 Corinthians 2:7-8 (NIV) "Now instead, you ought to forgive and comfort him, so that he will not be overwhelmed by excessive sorrow. I urge you, therefore, to reaffirm your love for him."

The Bible tells us to forgive an offender, one who has caused grief. How much more should we be willing to forgive our own husbands? Even a godly man is not without faults or imperfections. It is most likely that your husband, indeed, needs your forgiveness, maybe even on a weekly basis, or more. Husbands do silly things sometimes that hurt us without them even knowing it. Forgiveness does not require the other's involvement. You can forgive someone without their acknowledgment, apology, or consent. Forgiveness is a choice that you get to make that frees you! Holding on to grievances will only cause bitterness and strife to grow. If your husband has grieved you, learn how to forgive Him as God has forgiven you. Just think how many chances God has given you. I know I am on, like, my millionth chance, so I try to show that same grace to my husband. Now, I know some grievances are bigger than others, but that doesn't change the point of forgiveness. Forgiveness can be given at all levels, some just require different physical actions, such as having to remove yourself from a harmful relationship, but forgiveness remains the same and can even be given from a distance if necessary.

Prayer:

Lord, I give You all of my hurt and bitterness. Right now, I forgive my husband of his wrongs and I pray he forgives me of mine. I understand no one is perfect and want to reaffirm my love for my husband and am asking You to help me do so. In Jesus's name, amen.

27

Restoration of Hearts

Galatians 6:1 (NIV) "Brothers and sisters, if someone is caught in a sin, you who live by the Spirit should restore that person gently."

Now, I do not know what you have done in the lifetime of your marriage or what your husband has done. Maybe you hurt him or maybe he hurt you. Maybe you broke his trust or he broke your trust. What matters now is restoration. God can restore our hearts toward our husbands and our husbands' hearts toward us. He does this through love, faith, and hope. God is the best heart surgeon I know, and while you or your husband's heart may be hardened toward one another, God can restore the love you once had for him and the love he once had for you. Have faith in God and His ability to restore. He is, after all, in the restoration business. Did he not restore our rightful place as His sons and daughters? Put your hope and trust in God concerning marriage. Let Him operate on your heart with the scalpel of the Word, and allow healing to take place within your marriage and heart. God can restore even the bleakest of marriages. Give God full reign of your heart and He will restore it to an even better condition than it was before. He can even restore the years that were stolen! (Joel 2:25) God can restore your love for your husband and your husband's love for you!

Prayer:

Lord, restore my heart and my husband's heart. Operate on both of us so that both of us can grow and are restored together in unity and are in one accord. In Jesus's name, amen.

28

Break Down Walls

Ezekiel 34:27 (NIV) "The trees will yield their fruit and the ground will yield its crops; the people will be secure in their land. They will know that I am the LORD, when I break the bars of their yoke and rescue them from the hands of those who enslaved them."

Personal walls. We all have them, we all build them. Some of our walls tower higher than others, but nonetheless, we build them to protect ourselves, or at least that is what we tell ourselves we are doing. I know I have personally built up walls against my husband thinking I was protecting myself and our marriage, because if he could not get to me emotionally, then I would never be hurt by him emotionally. But the thing about walls is that they work both ways. My husband could not reach me and I could not reach him because I built up a barrier between us that was actually hurting our marriage, not protecting it, or me. I had to decide to let God . . .LET GOD . . . break down my walls. In marriage, walls are not your protection; God is your protection. Sometimes we have ancient walls from previous experiences and relationships that are blocking and hindering the growth of our marriage. You may think that wall is protecting you, but in reality, it's

61

blocking you. Give God permission to tear down any wall that you have built against your husband.

Prayer:

Lord, break down any walls that stand between me and my husband. Help me to see when I am starting to build a wall against him as well so that I may find my protection in You and not in my coping mechanism. I give You permission to bring down the walls in my marriage. In Jesus's name, amen.

29

Voiceless

Micah 7:7 (NIV) "But as for me, I watch in hope for the LORD, I wait for God my Savior; my God will hear me."

There are times in marriage where you just don't feel heard. I know. I've been there. It's like your voice, your opinion, does not even matter. My husband has asked me my opinion only to go do exactly what he wanted to do the next day (nothing bad, just didn't agree with my opinion) and that's okay, it just does not always feel okay. When a husband does not listen to his wife, it can feel like Ursula from *The Little Mermaid* stole her voice and she's just there trying to talk, but nothing comes out . . .or like on the reality television show, *The Voice*, when a singer is belting their heart out and none of the judges press their buttons to turn around. It's a very humiliating and empty feeling, like your voice does not count. But I want to end that notion right here, right now. The fact is your voice does matter. You are heard! Maybe not by your husband, but by someone much bigger than him. God hears you. He hears you every time you speak to Him, actually. Not only does He hear, but He truly listens and does not ignore you, and He gives great feedback and advice! No matter what, you need to know that God will hear you, so when your husband just does not seem to get it, or flat-out does not listen, or care, run to God, for He hears you and knows your heart better than you know it yourself. Let your confidence be in the fact that God hears you!

Prayer:

Lord, when I feel voiceless and like my husband does not care, teach me to run to You and talk to You because I know You hear my voice. I pray that through the feeling of not being heard that my prayer life grows so that I know You hear me and that I am heard by who matters most. In Jesus's name, amen.

30

Not Alone

Matthew 28:20 (NIV) "And surely I am with you always, to the very end of the age."

Jesus was speaking to His disciples when He said this and it was to reassure them that He would always be with them even when they could not see Him. He wanted to let them know that even after He ascended that He would be there to help them and guide them while they did His work. Marriage, in and of itself, is a ministry, and an important one at that. You are not alone in marriage or as a wife. God is right there with you, by your side, teaching you, helping you, and guiding you. My finite mind can't comprehend how He is always there for each one of us, but He is, and He does not fail. Take a deep breath today and remember who is walking right alongside you in your marriage. Yes, it's you and your husband, but God is there too. Stride for stride. Step for step. Count on Him to be there. Through the tears of sorrow and for every victory, God is there. Maybe you just needed that reminder today . . . that God is with you, He sees you, He knows you by name, and everything is going to be okay. You are not alone!

Prayer:

Lord, remind me of Your presence in my marriage, in my home, and in my life. Never let me forget that You are there through the good and the bad. I know I can count on You and that You have never left me or forsaken me! In Jesus's name, amen.

31

Just Beautiful

1 Peter 3:3-4 (NIV) "Your beauty should not come from outward adornment, such as elaborate hairstyles and the wearing of gold jewelry or fine clothes. Rather, it should be that of your inner self, the unfading beauty of a gentle and quiet spirit, which is of great worth in God's sight."

The world places a lot of emphasis on beauty, and wives are held to this impossible standard to look good all the time. Some men even want those "trophy wives." Culture can't even accept the fact that women age either. Can't we age gracefully without disrespect? I want to just yell out to the world and say, "Hey, news flash, everyone grows old if they are so blessed to live long enough." Wrinkles happen. Gravity happens. Stretchmarks happen. Because . . . of a thing I like to call *life*. God set a different standard for beauty and it's crucial for women to see themselves through His mirror and not the world's mirror. *Who are you?* That question cannot be answered by anything physical because who you are is not what you look like; who you are is who God created you to be. God finds beauty in the inner self of a person, a beauty that won't fade because of time. Wives, yes, you should strive to be healthy and take care of yourself physically. Fix your hair, brush your teeth, be healthy so you can be around longer, but know that God's definition of beauty is not that. God says who you are as a person, gentleness, and quietness are what make you beautiful. As a Christian wife your beauty goes much deeper than skin and you are beautiful!

Prayer:

Lord, help me to see beauty that is deeper than outward appearances and help me see the qualities in myself that You call beautiful. Open my husband's heart and eyes to see my true beauty as well, so our bond is not just purely physical but spiritual. In Jesus's name, amen.

32

Truly Loved

1 John 4:16 (NIV) "And so we know and rely on the love God has for us. God is love. Whoever lives in love lives in God, and God in them."

Know love, give love, receive love . . . Pretty simple concept when you think about it. Once we know love, we are able to give love, and because we have given love it is proof that we have received love. God says that we love because He first loved us. It is God's love that sustains us. Christian wives need to know that they are truly loved—that God loves them perfectly, deeply, and wholly. There is no emptiness in God's love. Once secure in God's love, a wife can show her husband that same love. Your husband needs love just like you do. Now, he may not show the need for it like you do, but God created everyone to crave love because He is love. If you do not have the love of the Father, how can you truly love? Make it your life's mission to rely on the love of God and show forth that love to all who encounter you, especially your husband. Love your husband truly, madly, and deeply and see where it takes your marriage. That God-given love you have can shape your marriage because it is patient, kind, does not boast, or envy. True love endures. As you show love and admiration to your husband, let him reciprocate that love for you. Let him know that he is truly loved and know you are truly loved too!

Prayer:

Lord, help me to show my husband true love, the type of love that You have shown me. I pray I know love, give love, and receive love as You would want me to. In Jesus's name, amen.

33

Reconstructed Trust

Psalm 111:7 (NIV) "The works of his hands are faithful and just; all his precepts are trustworthy."

This scripture is referring to God. The works of God's hands are faithful and just and He is trustworthy. As Christians, we strive to be like Him and trustworthiness is admirable, especially in marriage. I want my husband to be able to trust me and I want to be able to trust him. Trust is fragile in the fact that it takes years to build, yet one moment to destroy. If you or your spouse have done something to break the trust in marriage then there needs to be some reconstruction that goes on, and this can only be successfully done through God, His Word, and prayer. I always tell my son to be a man of integrity, someone who is the same behind closed doors as he is in front of a crowd, and I think that's what we need to be—husbands and wives of integrity. If you were the one to break your husband's trust, ask for forgiveness and go beyond words to show your husband that he can once again trust you. All you can do is your end of things . . . if he broke trust, be quick to forgive and slow to anger, and go to God in whom you know you can trust beyond a shadow of a doubt concerning your marriage. God can rebuild your trust in your spouse. Give Him the time to do so and trust Him through the process of reconstruction.

Prayer:

Lord, reconstruct the trust within my marriage. Repair the damage we have done and as we trust You, reconstruct our trust in our marriage. I trust You with my heart, I trust You with my husband, and I trust You with our marriage. In Jesus's name, amen.

34

Marriage is Honorable

Hebrews 13:4 (NIV) "Marriage should be honored by all."

When you entered into marriage, you entered into an honorable union, one that should be a blessing and representation of Christ's love. Don't let what others say, or what the world says, define your marriage. Your marriage deserves better than that. In the sight of God, your marriage is a covenant between you, your spouse, and Him. It's a promise that is sacred and should be honored by both you and your husband. Do not let anyone disrespect your union with your spouse. Don't speak negatively about your marriage to others. If you need help, find the proper outlet, such as godly counseling. By honoring your marriage, you are honoring God. Your marriage is to be honest, moral, ethical, and righteous. Be a wife of integrity and keep the sanctity of your marriage holy. When the world tries to misrepresent God's plan for your marriage, go to the Word and remember marriage should be honored by all.

Prayer:

Lord, my heart is to honor You with my marriage. Give me an honorable relationship with my husband and let us both be an example of Your love and covenant. In Jesus's name, amen.

35

Your Role Matters

Proverbs 31:17 (NIV) "She sets about her work vigorously…"

Your husband is blessed to have you in his life! Wives do so much in a marriage and it can sometimes be overlooked, but I want you to know that your role matters. Without a wife there can be no husband and without a husband there can be no wife. Without the first man, Adam, there would be no woman as the woman was taken from the man's rib and woman gives birth to man, so one is not more significant than the other (1 Corinthians 11:12). Each has their own importance within marriage. God designed both of us to compliment the other, not hinder. As a wife, you are not under your husband's feet, you are at his side. Woman came from the rib after all and not the foot. God has always shown that a woman's role matters. Whether you do all of the domestic duties or you pay all of the bills doesn't really matter. What matters is that you honor God and your husband. What works for one couple may not work for the other. Talk to your spouse and figure out what honors God and works for both of you. And remember, letting your husband lead does not make you weak, or devalue your position as the wife. It means you trust him. God made the role of wife important!

Prayer:

Lord, remind me that I play a big part in the success of my marriage and that my role matters. Help my husband and me honor You and find out what works for both of us. In Jesus's name, amen.

36

Give, Give, Give

Acts 20:35 (ESV) "In all things I have shown you that by working hard in this way we must help the weak and remember the words of the Lord Jesus, how he himself said, 'It is more blessed to give than to receive.'"

We have heard it said many times by our mothers, fathers, grandmothers, etc. since we have been young, that it is better to give than it is to receive. Operating at this level of maturity in marriage takes hard work and discipline on the part of the giver. The giver must learn to give without expecting anything in return, although there *is* great reward in giving. The giver must not hold any resentment toward the receiver after they have given. The giver is an example of Christ-like love and devotion. It may seem, or you may feel, that in your marriage you're always the one to give, give, give, but God blesses those who give of themselves. The giver must continually be seeking God and His righteousness to live in a perpetual state of giving without getting burnt out. How can you pour from an empty vessel? You can't. You can't operate on zero percent, so make sure you are full and replenished in the Lord and He will help you be a giver in your marriage.

Prayer:

Lord, make me a giver in my relationship with my husband. Fill me up so that I may be a blessing in my marriage without running myself into the ground. Teach me when, how, and where I can give more in my marriage and to my spouse and give me supernatural rest to replenish my mental and physical body as You replenish my spirit. In Jesus's name, amen.

37

The Sacrifice

Hebrews 13:16 (ESV) "Do not neglect to do good and to share what you have, for such sacrifices are pleasing to God."

Most of us in a marriage know what it is to do good within that marriage, and how to share with our spouses the intimate parts of our lives that no one else gets to see. But sometimes, it's not easy to do good and we don't want to share what we have with our husbands for one reason or another. Maybe we are not in the mood, maybe we want to be left alone, maybe we are just plain exhausted. (And no, I am not referring to or hinting at sex, although it might fit here too.) I am talking about the sacrifice of what we want so that we can do good unto our husbands and sacrifice a bit of self to really pay attention to our husbands. I am talking about emotional and physical availability to our spouses. For example, my husband loves to go out to eat, but I prefer to be at home, so sometimes I sacrifice what I want to spend time with him and vice versa. Sometimes he will bring something home instead. When you get married, it stops being about what you want all the time. Now, there is another involved. Marriage is a mutual sacrifice, meaning there will be times when you give up what you want for the other because you love them, and I believe such sacrifices in marriage (by both parties) honor God.

Prayer:

Lord, help me to not neglect doing good in my marriage and help me to share with my husband as well as help him to share with me and do good for our relationship too. I pray I am not selfish but am willing to learn to sacrifice in a Biblical way so that my marriage will benefit from it. In Jesus's name, amen.

38

Personal Growth

2 Peter 3:18 (NIV) "But grow in the grace and knowledge of our Lord and Savior Jesus Christ. To him be glory both now and forever! Amen."

There is never a time to stop growing. As long as there is breath in your lungs, there is room to grow in life and in marriage. Even after fourteen years, I am still learning new things about my husband. 1) Because I am older and wiser, and I see things differently. 2) Because he is older and his personal tastes have changed. 3) Because every day is different and new, you never know what life has in store. As such, it is important to always be growing and allowing God to shape you. A spouse's personal growth often results in marital growth, where you apply what you have learned about yourself to fortify and strengthen your relationship. Grow in the Lord and in your understanding of His Word and your marriage will undoubtedly be blessed in return. Marriage has been described as a triangle with God at the highest point; the closer you both get to God, the closer you both become. If your husband is yet to be saved, then you grow and get closer to God and let God use you as an example of how He transforms, shapes, and helps those who love Him.

Prayer:

Lord, I want to grow in the grace and knowledge of Your Word and in Jesus Christ. Use my growth in You to shape who I am in my marriage and use me to show my husband Your goodness. In Jesus's name, amen.

39

The Diligent Wife

Proverbs 31:13 (NIV) "She selects wool and flax and works with eager hands."

The word "diligent" comes from the Latin word *"diligere"* and means to value highly or to take delight in. In English, it means careful and hardworking. As we see this verse is found in Proverbs 31, which is the gold standard for a Christian wife. Whether you are a stay-at-home wife or mother, or work part-time or full-time, makes no difference in the level of diligence that you give. If you stay at home, you have the opportunity to be diligent in the home while your husband works. Your work at home is just as important as his paying job. If you work too, and help financially provide, your diligence in your work is just as important as his too. As Christian wives, we should highly value what we do and who we are. God created us to be "help meets," meaning we help our husbands when and where we can. Often times, women are the better multitaskers, and this is an innate trait I believe God gave women to help them as wives and mothers. If you are like me, multitasking may not be your strong suit, but you can still be diligent with what you do right where you are. Care about your work and your work will shine!

Prayer:

Lord, make my hands eager to work where You want me to work. Teach me and my husband how to appreciate the work that I do inside and outside of the home. In Jesus's name, amen.

40

Bringing out the Best in Your Husband

Proverbs 31:12 (NIV) "She brings him good, not harm, all the days of her life."

I want you to know that being a Proverbs 31 wife/woman is not unattainable, although I know sometimes it seems that way. Here's another verse used to help wives see their full potential. You can bring out the best in your husband, and, yes, he should strive to bring out the best in you too. Remember, you are both on the same team. As you encourage him and bring out the best in him, something should spark in him to want to do the same for you. You get what you give and what you put in is what you see come out. If you are always bringing your husband good, then sooner or later, he is going to recognize that and see you as a blessing in his life. Is there something your husband does well? Don't hesitate to tell him so! I have a challenge for you. Start giving your husband compliments and pointing out the things he does well. Will his face light up? I bet it does, because everyone loves a compliment, especially from someone they love and who matters to them. Your opinion of your spouse matters to your spouse. I have never met a husband who did not like his wife saying something nice about him! So, go on, and bring your husband good and not harm all the days of your life, because you rock and have the ability to brighten his whole world!

Prayer:

Lord, I want to bring good and not harm to my husband, show me how I can do this and make me a blessing to my husband by bringing out the best in him. In Jesus's name, amen.

41

Date Night

Genesis 2:18 (KJV) "And the Lord God said, 'It is not good that the man should be alone; I will make him a help meet for him.'"

Okay, let's get real. When was the last time you and your husband had a nice romantic date, just you and him? You see, married couples should never stop dating because they were made for each other—a wife for her husband and a husband for his wife. They belong together and date night reminds both of them of this. Put the phone away and go out with your hubby, you know, that person you said "I do" to; yeah him! Enjoy him. Talk to him. Get to know him all over again. The dishes can wait, laundry will be waiting for you when you get back, the to-do list is not going anywhere. Maybe a "real" date night out is not possible because of lack of a babysitter or finances, but who says date night can't be right in your own living room? I mean, kids eventually do go to sleep, right, leaving you and your hubby to enjoy the company of one another. Sit down and relax with the one you love and be present both physically and mentally. At the end of the day, outside of your relationship with Christ, the most important relationship you have is with your spouse. Nurture and cultivate your love for him by setting time aside for him at least once a week for a date night both you and he deserve.

Prayer:

Lord, help me to be my husband's helpmate and let us both make time for each other, and make each other a priority. Let me never take for granted my husband or the time I have with him. In Jesus's name, amen.

42

Strong Enough

Proverbs 31:17 (NIV) "...her arms are strong for her tasks."

Do you know how someone becomes strong enough to lift more than their own body weight? Training. Lots and lots of training. The more you work on your strength, the stronger you will become. Right now, you may not feel like a strong enough wife, but I am telling you that God will give you the strength that you need in your marriage. God will train your spiritual arms to be strong to hold your husband and your children. He will give you the stamina and make you strong enough for every task a wife must tackle. Your training ground is not at the gym, but on your knees with your eyes on the Word of God. You are stronger than you know and can do more for your marriage than you give yourself credit. Go, and set about your work vigorously; your arms are strong enough for your family. Keep training and keep fighting for your faith because your husband and children need you, and your prayers, and your strength. You are strong enough! No one can take care of your family like you can! Your husband can walk alongside you in life but only God can carry you through. You've got this because God's got you!

Prayer:

Lord, make my arms strong for my husband and family, and let me be a pillar of strength for them as You are my pillar of strength. Let them see where my strength comes from and that You are my source. In Jesus's name, amen.

43

Knowing Your Worth

Proverbs 31:10 (ESV) "An excellent wife who can find? She is far more precious than jewels."

As a wife, you add value to your husband. You add more to the marriage than you probably realize. God created women to be a source of strength for their husbands, and you are much stronger and more valuable than you give yourself credit for. We wives tend to discredit all that we do, belittling it or acting like it's not a big deal, but oh, it's a big deal! What you do adds so much worth to your marriage. Whether you are a working wife or a stay-at-home wife, what you bring to the table of marriage is invaluable. It takes both wife and husband to make a marriage work, and without one, there is not the other. Learn to acknowledge your worth in the relationship. God uniquely created you to be who you need to be for your spouse and He has placed worth on the inside of you. Your worth and value have already been assigned by God. Remember this verse and know that you are far more precious than jewels when it comes to your husband.

Prayer:

Lord, help me to see my worth within my marriage. Allow me to see where I can provide support for my husband and open my eyes to see what I can do within the relationship to better it and strengthen it. In Jesus's name, amen.

44

My Husband, My Friend

Proverbs 17:17 (KJV) "A friend loveth at all times . . . "

If you and your husband are not friends, my question to you is, why not? Your husband is the closest person to you, or at least, should be. What's stopping you from letting him be your friend? Friendship within marriage is part of the bond that ties you and your spouse together. Everyone needs companionship and the best place to get it in marriage is your spouse. My husband and I are different in a lot of ways, yet he is my best friend. I talk to him, laugh with him, and cry with him. We are not best friends because we have everything in common; we are best friends because we choose to be. A spouse can be that friend you need and will always be there for you. Have you made an effort to be friendly with your spouse? Another part of friendship is time, and who better to give your time to than your husband? (Other than God, of course.) Becoming your husband's best friend will allow both of you to grow closer together and will make the bond of marriage that much stronger. Your husband can be that friend you need! If you and your husband are already best friends, you're on the right track. Keep it up! Remember, friendship is as a foundation for Biblical love. To have your husband as your friend is a blessing to your marriage. And as the Word says, a friend loves at all times!

Prayer:

Lord, allow me and my husband to grow closer through friendship with one another, living, laughing, and spending time with one another, and help me to love him at all times. In Jesus's name, amen.

45

The Thoughtful Wife

Proverbs 31:15 (NIV) "She gets up while it is still night; she provides food for her family and portions for her female servants."

When I read this verse in Proverbs 31, I first see that this wife wakes up early to take care of her family, and not only does she take care of her family, but her servants too. That is a thoughtful woman. Is there anything that you could do in your marriage that would show your thoughtfulness? Think about your husband for a moment and ask yourself how you can be thoughtful toward him. Does he love coffee? Maybe wake up a little earlier and make him a cup just the way he likes it. Does he like a certain dish that you could make him for dinner? (Yes, I have heard that a way to a man's heart is through his stomach, so that is why both those examples are about food/beverages.) I can't cook (not great, anyway) and my husband does not like coffee, so sometimes I will get him something out of the blue that he has mentioned just because, or I will run an errand he would normally have to run. It really is not that hard to show a little extra thoughtfulness in your marriage, and by being thoughtful, you are showing your husband that you hear him, care for him, and are there for him.

Prayer:

Lord, make me more thoughtful in my marriage and show me something that I can do that will help my husband know how much I care for him. In Jesus's name, amen.

46

A Woman's Intuition

Proverbs 31:26 (NIV) "She speaks with wisdom, and faithful instruction is on her tongue."

Sometimes it is downright scary how a woman can sense/feel something before it ever happens. Women's intuition is said to be a myth, but maybe there is some truth to a woman who tries to understand what is going on around her. Beyond a shadow of a doubt, I know that the Spirit of God can guide a woman and direct her path, and marriage is not excluded from that! With the Holy Spirit's help and guidance, a Christian wife can discern a good deal from a bad one, she can discern what choice needs to be made, and can instruct her family to safety. God has given women the type of heart that can be compassionate and empathize with others. A Christian wife's intuition is invaluable to her husband. The counsel she gives is sound and God-led, which means she can help her husband make the right decisions too. Being a Christian wife comes with a lot of responsibility, but it also comes with a lot of honor as well. I pray you have godly intuition that will help your marriage and your family. Speak with wisdom and instruct in faith!

Prayer:

Lord, give me the power to discern and help me to make the right choices for myself, husband, and family. As You guide and direct my heart, let me share wisdom with my spouse that only You could give me. In Jesus's name, amen.

47

Stand by Your Man

1 Corinthians 7:10-11 (ESV) "To the married I give this charge (not I, but the Lord): the wife should not separate from her husband (but if she does, she should remain unmarried or else be reconciled to her husband), and the husband should not divorce his wife."

I don't want to focus on the word "divorce" for this devotion even though it is part of the passage I am quoting, but what I do want to do is look at how the verse says a wife should not separate from her husband. Wives can detach from their husbands in other ways besides divorce, so we ought to be careful. There are a lot of wives who separate from their husbands without divorcing them and without leaving them; they just become distant within the relationship. The only way marriage can work is if you try. Not trying equals not working. Through thick and thin, stand by your man, just as he should stand by you. Marriage is sacred and your relationship with your husband should not be trivial. Stand by him when he is sick and when he is well. Stand by him when he has nothing and when he has everything. Just stand by him. No one said marriage was easy. Standing by your man will show him just how much you love him for who he is and not what he has.

(Disclaimer: I know the day in which we live might twist some things around, so I want to be clear. No, I do not agree with standing by your man if he abuses you, so please seek the help needed and protect yourself. I believe you are still honoring God when you move yourself out of harm's way.)

Prayer:

Lord, I pray for the strength to stand by my husband through thick and thin, and that he has the courage to stand by me no matter what comes. Help us to both learn to trust and count on each other the way You would have us to do so. In Jesus's name, amen.

48

The Creative Wife

Proverbs 31:24 (NIV) "She makes linen garments and sells them, and supplies the merchants with sashes."

You may be asking yourself, "How does this passage of scripture apply to the 21st century?" I know there are no merchants to supply sashes to outside of your door and that you may not be a seamstress, so selling linen clothes is out of the picture, but what I see in this verse is that the Proverbs 31 woman was creative in the way she did business. She did what she could, with what she had, and did something with it. As a Christian wife, you can be creative right where you are and use your time and talents to do something productive. I believe God would have every Christian wife to be productive because idle hands lead to ruin. There are just so many hours in the day that you can fill with doing something great, like working to make your dreams to become reality, spending time with your husband, or cherishing your children. You can be creative and do what makes you happy while still being a godly wife! Dream, live, and love!

Prayer:

Lord, make me creative with the spare time that I have.
Show me ways that I can be creative that will bless me
and my family in return. In Jesus's name, amen,

49

Saved, Fierce, & Fabulous

Proverbs 31:25 (NIV) "She is clothed with strength and dignity; she can laugh at the days to come."

How nice would it be if we, as Christian wives, could laugh at the days to come? I often ask myself, "How could the Proverbs 31 woman laugh at the days to come?" I mean the days to come, especially in our future, are not funny, not something to really laugh about. The Lord showed me that she can laugh because she knows the truth, she can laugh because she took the time to prepare for her family, she can laugh because she knows who God is—to her and her family. She can laugh because, in the end, she wins. My dear sister in Christ, clothe yourself with strength and dignity. Jesus is coming again and He is looking for a bride who is ready. Share with your husband the time in which we live and always be pointing to Christ and His return. Prepare your heart, know the truth, remember how big your God is, and know that one day, when it is all said and done, you win because you served the Lord first in your life. You, Christian wife, are saved by grace, fierce with the Word, and fabulous in marriage!

Prayer:

Lord, remind me every day that I am saved, fierce, and fabulous and can laugh at the days to come because I know who You are! In Jesus's name, amen.

50

The Overseer

Proverbs 31:27 (NIV) "She watches over the affairs of her household and does not eat the bread of idleness."

Have you ever had a sick day, where you can't get out of bed, and noticed that your household did not function quite the way it should without you? Men are great leaders, and our husbands are called by God to be spiritual leaders of the home, but wives tend to see to the everyday affairs of the home more so than the husband (not always). I'm not talking gender roles because I know men can do domestic duties too, but in Proverbs 31, it clearly says that this wife oversees her home and is not idle within the home. As a Christian wife, you most likely have the best perspective of the ins-and-outs and ebbs-and-flows of your home and the way it works. Keeping schedules, making appointments, and securing the home to make sure it runs properly is a high-level task and no woman should be ashamed of it. You are as an overseer of the home and if you were to get paid, it would be a lot. Praise God for the godly wives who run the household well; they are the glue of the family and their children shall rise up and call her blessed!

Prayer:

Lord, make me a good overseer of our home. Help me with all that I have to do and give me the fortitude and foresight I need to make my home great. In Jesus's name, amen.

51

Untouchable

Mark 10:8-9 (KJV) "Wherefore they are no more twain, but one flesh. What therefore God hath joined together, let not man put asunder."

Have you ever wished for a marriage that was unmistakably untouchable? The type of marriage that NO ONE and NOTHING could touch or hinder? The type of marriage that was "ride or die"? Do those types of marriages even exist? Yes, but not without a whole lot of effort put into them. You and your husband become as one flesh after marriage and it is both of your responsibilities to fight on behalf of the marriage, the unity, and each other. When my husband "goes to bat" for me, I feel so loved and confident. From what I have seen, most husbands would fight to defend their wives and that's how it should be. Husbands and wives are to defend one another, stand by the other's side, and protect the other. Let NO MAN come between you and YOUR MAN. Avoid any inappropriate conduct or attachment to other men, or even hobbies that are unhealthily separating you from your spouse. Life is a balancing act and so is marriage. Make sure you are prioritizing the right things in the right order. I have learned that God is ALWAYS first, then my husband, then my children, then my extended family, then other things. My first priority is to be a godly woman and have that aspect of my life flow into everything else I do. An untouchable marriage is not impossible. With God, all things are possible; you just have to give Him the faith and commitment to work with.

Prayer:

Lord, I pray that my marriage is untouchable and that what You have joined together no man can put asunder. Remove any unhealthy habit or relationships in my life that are hindering my marriage and work on my husband's heart so that he will do the same. In Jesus's name, amen.

52

A Considerate Wife

Proverbs 31:16 (NIV) "She considers a field and buys it; out of her earnings she plants a vineyard."

When I think of a considerate person, I think of their willingness to think and care about others. I believe a considerate wife is someone who thinks, cares, and behaves in a way that shows that others are important to her. My mom is one of the most considerate people I know. She thinks of others before herself and, from her, I have learned that being considerate is an important part of marriage. To be a considerate wife would mean to think of your spouse and how he would feel in certain situations. Again, it's putting yourself in his shoes, and as we see in this verse in Proverbs 31, she also considers her purchases and her responsibilities. She considered the field before she bought it. She put her earnings toward something that would benefit not only her but her family. Now, I am a shopper. God has delivered me from a shopping addiction and taught me how to consider before I buy. Everything you do as a wife can be done considerately and God will show you how. Consider your husband, your children, and your family and see how your actions might impact their lives. Give thought to your actions!

Prayer:

Lord, make me a considerate wife and help me to think about my actions and how it impacts my marriage and my family. I want to be a blessing and for my decisions to make a positive impact in other's lives. In Jesus's name, amen.

53

Pillar of Faith

Matthew 17:20 (NIV) "Truly I tell you, if you have faith as small as a mustard seed, you can say to this mountain, 'Move from here to there,' and it will move. Nothing will be impossible for you."

Faith is the substance of things hoped for, the evidence of things unseen (Hebrews 11:1). Faith changes everything. When you have faith as a wife, your whole marriage can be transformed, renewed, rejuvenated, restored. If your marriage needs it, you can pray for it in faith and watch God work like only He can. All God needs to be able to work in your life and in your marriage is YOUR FAITH. Faith as small as a mustard seed can move mountains! If you really believe and you apply faith to your marriage then you will see God's hand in your marriage. Give God your husband. Any woes, any grievances you have against your husband, I challenge you to give them to God and become a pillar of faith for your marriage. Whether you have been married a day or twenty years, faith can and will only improve your marriage and relationship with your husband. Faith gives you an undeniable hope that says, "We're 'gonna' make it." Pillar of faith, it's time to move those mountains in your marriage.

Prayer:

Lord, increase my faith right now as I pray for my husband. Transform our marriage into what You want it to be. Make me a pillar of faith in my marriage and let me see, with my own eyes, the mountains move. In Jesus's name, amen.

54

Worthwhile

Proverbs 31:30-31 (NIV) ". . . but a woman who fears the Lord is to be praised. Honor her for all that her hands have done, and let her works bring her praise at the city gate."

I know that the majority of these devotions require a lot from you and place a lot of challenges on your role as a wife, but then I see this verse and understand that it is all worth it. All the work you are putting in to better your relationship with your spouse will be worth it. These scriptures you have been applying to your marriage are worthy investments that will not return void, because the Word of God does not fail, not ever! You will see honor and respect come to you. As you fear the Lord and follow His commands, your husband will surely notice. He will notice the consideration, love, and kindness. It may take time as most things do, but you will be honored for your diligence. If you have children, they will see it too and will rise up and call you blessed. They will see the work of the Lord in your life and when you are old and gray, you can lean back and know that all you had done in faith for your marriage and family was worthwhile. So keep praying, keep striving, and keep fighting for faith, Christian wife, it will all be worth it in the end.

Prayer:

Lord, allow the work of my hands to bring praise at the city gate. Make me realize that all of my hard work is worthwhile and that my honor is found in You. In Jesus's name, amen.

55

Biggest Fan

Luke 6:31 (NIV) "Do to others as you would have them do to you."

I am not much of a sports fanatic but I do know that during the Super Bowl, people go crazy for their team—donning all the gear, painting their faces, and even waving gigantic #1 foam fingers. Fans cheer and roar when their team is winning and doing well, and I realized that's how I should feel about my husband. I should be his #1 fan, the biggest, the "baddest," the "bestest" (I know, not real words) fan he has ever seen. I may not don a shirt with his name on it, or paint my face (although I do wear makeup, does that count?), or wear a giant foam finger, but I do want to show him that I support him and his endeavors, even if they're a little out there. I say dream big! I would expect him to be my biggest fan too, and he is and has been. There is just something about your spouse's support that makes you feel more capable, like you could conquer the world because you have this fan who believes in you. So, Christian wife, will you be your husband's biggest fan? Roar for him. Cheer for him. Root him on. Let him know that there's not a fan out there like you because you're his biggest fan!

Prayer:

Lord, make me a wife that roots for her husband and cheers him on. Help me to be the encourager he needs in his life. In Jesus's name, amen.

56

Giving it Your All

1 Peter 4:8 (NIV) "Above all, love each other deeply, because love covers a multitude of sins."

There have been times in my marriage where I was just completely depleted and I recognized that I was not giving my marriage my all. I didn't know how to get the energy, drive, or "want to" to get back to it. I mean, I was drained physically, emotionally, and mentally. So maybe now you're asking, "Well, what did you do to give it your all again?" I wish there was a magic answer, one that would be more satisfying, but the truth is I had to recharge myself in the Lord through what I am always supposed to do: pray, read the Word, worship, and praise. You know when I can't give my all is when I have not been seeking God as I ought to and I was drained because I never recharged. To give marriage your all requires you to give your all to God. I had to pray. I had to praise. And I had to PUSH. Push myself to be who God wanted me to be and not who it was easy to be. It's easy to be a lazy wife who does not love the other deeply, but it takes a woman of God who sees what it takes to push through and love her husband deeply, so deeply that she could see past his faults as God sees us through the blood of Christ. Christian wife, if you are drained, it's time to fill up. Get into the Word of God, eat of it, and charge up. You've got a whole lot of loving yet to do.

Prayer:

Lord, when I feel empty, give me the wherewithal to come and be recharged in You. Give my mind, body, and soul supernatural rest so that I may love at full throttle. Recharge me, Lord. In Jesus's name, amen.

57

Fix Me

Psalm 51:10 (NIV) "Create in me a pure heart, O God, and renew a steadfast spirit within me."

Oh man, as I studied to write this devotion, it wrecked me as a wife because so often I want to pray, "Lord, fix my husband," when I need some "fixin" done myself. It's really easy for me to point out all the areas in my husband that I wished would improve, but when it comes to him pointing out what he wished I would improve on it gets a little tense. Whenever my primary attitude is "If he would just fix what I want him to fix then there would be no problem." With that attitude, I am opting out of responsibility and accountability. Every time I reject feedback from my husband concerning my behavior, I force my husband to shoulder my share of responsibility as well as his own. A lack of humility is a surefire way to alienate a husband and put strain on a relationship. I learned that being a know-it-all solves nothing, so yes, I pray for my husband's heart and that the Lord would soften him in certain areas, but I added to my prayer, "Lord, fix me, and fix my heart." That prayer is not near as much fun to pray because instead of seeing the changes in my husband, I see the areas that I need to work on and it can be hard to see where I have been at fault and wrong in my marriage. I don't like being wrong, but in some areas, I was . . . am . . . I'm a work in progress. What about you? Are there any areas in your marriage that you can pray the "Lord, fix me and my heart" prayer?

Prayer:

Lord, fix me. If there are any hardened places on my heart in my marriage, I pray that You remove them. Soften my heart toward my husband and show me the areas in my life that I can improve and work on. In Jesus's name, amen.

58

Lean on God

Proverbs 3:5-6 (ESV) "Trust in the Lord with all your heart, and do not lean on your own understanding. In all your ways acknowledge him, and he will make straight your paths."

There has never been a time in my marriage where I could have done it on my own. I have always needed to trust in God. Even on my wedding day, I had to trust God that this was the man that I was supposed to spend the rest of my life with, that he would cherish me, love me, and provide for me. I was very young when I got married, so I was very much dependent on God for my future. In marriage, you must fully trust God, with your whole heart. You can't lean on your own understanding because it will fail you. You can only understand so much, but God, He sees the beginning from the end and He knows what you need, when you need it. Lean on HIM. Acknowledge God in your marriage and He will make the path straight. Even if your husband does not know God like you do, you can invite God into your marriage and that will make a difference. Remember, it's not about what you see; it's about what God can do! Lean on God. He's got you.

Prayer:

Lord, when I can't see how things are going to work out,
I trust You. Help me to not lean on my own
understanding but onto Yours. In Jesus's name, amen.

59

The Virtue of Patience

Proverbs 16:32 (NIV) "Better a patient person than a warrior, one with self-control than one who takes a city."

You know how they say patience is a virtue? After fourteen years of marriage and two kids, I believe them. The Bible says that a person with patience is better than a warrior! *A warrior*! Sign me up. I've always wanted to be better than a warrior. How about you? Yet, that's easier said than done. Do you know who I lose my patience with the most? The ones closest to me. Both my husband and my children have felt my wrath. It's not pretty (just ask them). In marriage, it seems so easy to lose patience with your husband, but if you can maintain self-control, you are better than one who can take an entire city! That sounds pretty victorious to me. Learn what is worth the fight and what isn't. Not everything has to escalate. Gain self-control and practice patience in your marriage and see where it gets you. I bet it gets you a lot farther than you ever expected. If love has to be represented as a battlefield, it is the cooler head that will prevail. Stay calm and show your patience. You are better than a warrior!

Prayer:

Lord, give me patience for my husband and family. Help me to practice self-control in every area of my life, including my marriage. In Jesus's name, amen.

60

Unconditional Love

John 15:12 (ESV) "This is my commandment, that you love one another as I have loved you."

I've got a question for you . . . Do you love your husband like Christ has loved you? Love is this crazy thing that God has given us that is so strong and undeniable. Love is truly extraordinary and not of this world. God is love and everything He does for us is based on love and done in love. His example makes it seem impossible to love my husband like He loves me, but if He told me to do it, then He will give me the strength to do it. God's love is unconditional, so how should we love our husbands? *Unconditionally.* If more husbands and wives would love each other unconditionally there would be a whole lot fewer divorces. Unconditional love is love without conditions, affection without limitations. While we are still human, I know that this love is hard to give, but I challenge you to love like this in your marriage. Love like this in your life. Just love. Because love is what will shine in the darkness. Love will stand against the odds, challenge the statistics, and break down barriers. Love is the strongest force on earth. God is love.

Prayer:

Lord, make me love like You love. Make the type of love that I have respond like the type of love You have for me. Give me the courage to love my husband unconditionally. In Jesus's name, amen.

61

The Big Picture

1 Corinthians 13:12 (NLT) "Now we see things imperfectly, like puzzling reflections in a mirror, but then we will see everything with perfect clarity. All that I know now is partial and incomplete, but then I will know everything completely, just as God now knows me completely."

At the end of the day, there's this big picture, a grand one that God has painted. Since the fall of man, God has been painting and restoring that which was lost. He paints a picture that shows marriage between one man and woman, a couple that loves each other and cherishes one another. A picture where the home is a place that is safe for both the husband and wife. Marriage is a place of comfort and security, of love and a place to belong. Right now, we can't see just what God meant for everything to be, but we can play a part in the big picture and be the Christian wives He wants us to be. No, marriage is not about gender roles, or who pays the bills, or who wears the proverbial "pants" in the family. No, marriage is a sanctity and covenant that God has given where love must endure. Christ often uses the relationship between the husband and wife as an example of Him and His bride, the church. There is a bigger picture and I want my marriage to honor God first and foremost. Your marriage is part of a bigger picture that honors God and can be an example to the world of His true love. (Read Hosea to see the intensity of God's love for us and how he used a husband's love/commitment for his wife to display this.)

Prayer:

Lord, I want my marriage to be part of a bigger picture, one that I may not be able to see, but that brings You honor and glory. I want my marriage to be one that displays true love and devotion. In Jesus's name, amen.

62

Vulnerability in Marriage

2 Corinthians 4:7 (ESV) "But we have this treasure in jars of clay, to show that the surpassing power belongs to God and not to us."

I think it is safe to say that most people hate to be vulnerable. I am not talking about being open to harm emotionally or physically, but I am talking about being open—open in a way with your husband that allows him to see the real you without any guards or barriers. One of the most important and freeing things you can do in your marriage is be honest, and honesty has a way of opening you up in a way that you might not normally do. Be open with your husband. Like this verse says, we have this treasure in jars of clay to show that the power belongs to God and not to us. I have always said that if you're vulnerable before God, you'll never be vulnerable (the "attack" type of vulnerable) before man. Take heed to those words and know that you will never be the type of vulnerable (where you are susceptible to harm or attack) in your marriage when you are completely vulnerable before God, because God is your refuge, a strong tower to run to, where you are safe. Vulnerability in marriage means being vulnerable before God and open with your husband. There is no need for walls in your marriage when God is your fortress.

Prayer:

Lord, make me vulnerable before You so that I am not vulnerable before man. Allow my heart to be open with my husband so that I may receive him without fear of harm or judgment. And I pray he knows that he can come to me too without fear of harm to his emotions. In Jesus's name, amen.

63

Accountable

Romans 14:12 (ESV) "So then each of us will give an account of himself to God."

Every single person on the face of this earth is responsible for their own actions. In marriage, you are only responsible for your own actions. You may not be able to control what your spouse does, but you have all the power to control what you do. In life, it's not always about what is done by others; it's about how you respond to what they do. If both spouses held themselves accountable to God first and each other second then there would be more successful marriages. Each one of us will give an account to God, so what is your account going to say? Let God hold you accountable within your marriage and relationship with your husband. Your hubby may be a great man or he may be a work in progress, but if your accountability is to God then there is no variation in your responsibility. You be the wife God has called you to be and let God work in your husband to make him the husband he was called to be. And then help hold each other accountable. Marriage takes two and the only thing you can do is your part; give the rest to God.

Prayer:

Lord, hold me accountable in my marriage and I pray for my husband's accountability in You too. I pray that we would both do our parts within our marriage to better it. I pray we are accountable to You first and accountable to each other second. In Jesus's name, amen.

64

Wife of Her Word

Deuteronomy 23:23 (ESV) "You shall be careful to do what has passed your lips, for you have voluntarily vowed to the Lord your God what you have promised with your mouth."

The most trustworthy people are those that are true to their word. Who would you count on . . . someone who backed out all the time, or someone who did exactly what they said they would do? Be a woman of your word. Let your actions line up with what you have said and let what you have said line up with your actions. Husbands need to be able to count on and depend on their wives to do what they said they would do. Keep your promises and let your words not be empty. One of the superpowers a wife has is the ability to keep her word. Your word should hold some weight because people know that when you say you're going to do something, you do it. By being a wife of your word, you are showing love, it's just in a different way. Can your husband trust what you say? Let your yes be yes and your no be no. Be a wife of your word!

Prayer:

Lord, make me a wife of my word. If I tell my husband I will do something, let me do it. Help me to be a promise keeper and build my husband's trust and confidence in what I say I will do. In Jesus's name, amen.

65

The Fearless Wife

1 John 4:18 (ESV) "There is no fear in love, but perfect love casts out fear. For fear has to do with punishment, and whoever fears has not been perfected in love."

God does not want us to be afraid, not in anything. He wants us to know that He is right there with us, even if we are walking through the valley of the shadow of death, we do not have to fear because He walks beside us. In marriage, God does not want you to be afraid. If you have any fear regarding your marriage or husband, allow God to remove that fear with His love. God's perfect love casts out all fear, even fear of commitment, or whatever the case may be within your marriage. The Bible also says that God has not given us the spirit of fear but of power, love, and a sound mind. God will give you a sound mind and take away those thoughts of fear when you meditate on His Word and His promises. Let your marriage be perfected in love and be the fearless wife, who knows God fights her battles. Fear does not belong in marriage. (If your husband is doing something to endanger your physical or emotional well-being and it causes you fear, please seek God and the proper help and stay safe.) Marriage is a place of love and freedom.

Christian wife, you do not have to fear. God has made you more than a conqueror through Christ! A fearless wife can take on whatever comes her way because she knows who goes before her. Be fearless in Him!

Prayer:

Lord, free me from any fears that I may have concerning my marriage and my husband. Give me power, love, and a sound mind in my marriage and make me a fearless wife. In Jesus's name, amen.

66

Wife after God's Heart

Matthew 6:33 (NIV) "But seek first his kingdom and his righteousness, and all these things will be given to you as well."

As wives, we often aim to please our husbands, but more importantly than pleasing our husbands, we must please God. Before we seek our own households, we must seek first the kingdom of God and His righteousness. Our obligation and commitment are to God first. When we seek Him first, we see that all the other things will be given to us as well. Sometimes we put our focus too much on the problem rather than the solution. God is the solution. He is the source from whom all blessings flow. Seek God first, and always, and He will meet the needs within your marriage. Any cracks in your relationship with your husband can be resolved, not by applying "spackle" yourself, but by going to God and letting Him fix it once and for all. We can't be Christian wives without God. Seek God's approval before seeking your husband's approval. Seek God's will before seeking your husband's will. God will never lead you astray and always has the answer. Be a wife after God's own heart and your entire family will be blessed by it.

Prayer:

Lord, I pray that I seek You first in all things. I put You first in my marriage and pray that I am a wife after Your own heart. In Jesus's name, amen.

67

Faithfulness

Proverbs 28:20 (ESV) "A faithful man will abound with blessings, but whoever hastens to be rich will not go unpunished."

Faithfulness . . . In marriage, that word has a whole lot of meaning. What exactly does faithfulness mean when it comes to the relationship with our husbands? It means to be faithful and not only in one area, but it means to be faithful physically, mentally, and emotionally too. Wives must be faithful to their husbands in body, mind, heart, and soul. So many marriages have been left in ruins because of unfaithfulness. When you said "I do" it was for life. Both you and your husband deserve the respect of the other being faithful. There should never be the question of whether or not you are faithful to your husband. If there is ever any room to stray or you feel yourself slipping away, take charge, call yourself out, and stop it before it begins. Your husband deserves faithfulness because faithfulness is what you both signed up for. The same faithfulness you expect from your spouse is the same faithfulness you should give. Be faithful to your vows and the promise you made. When you are faithful, you and your marriage will ABOUND with blessings.

Prayer:

Lord, I pray that I am a faithful wife—faithful in all areas: physically, emotionally, and mentally. Help me to give my husband the faithfulness he deserves. In Jesus's name, amen.

68

The Caretaker

Mark 10:44-45 (ESV) "And whoever would be first among you must be slave of all. For even the Son of Man came not to be served but to serve, and to give his life as a ransom for many."

Husbands should take care of their wives and wives should take care of their husbands. Marriage is not about being served, but rather serving the other, not as a slave, but as a willing vessel to be like Christ. You know when you are sick and someone looks after you, taking care of you, making sure you have what you need . . . doesn't that make you feel loved and cared for? Why is it that one of us has to be sick in marriage for the other to be a caretaker? We can take care of each other even if neither one of us is sick. Take care of your hubby in ways that you know how. If he is having a super stressed day, surprise him with his favorite meal or a shoulder massage, or just something to let him know that you are there to take care of him if he needs you or wants you to. Sometimes even the words, "Hey, you need me to do anything for you?" can be super comforting, even if he can't think of anything for you to do. At least you showed him you cared enough to ask. Jesus was all about service and taking care of others.

Marriage is not about being served but serving the other in love. Will you be the type of wife that takes care of her husband?

Prayer:

Lord, help me to take care of my husband as a willing vessel to show forth Your love in my marriage. In Jesus's name, amen.

69

Fight Free Zone

Proverbs 21:19 (ESV) "It is better to live in a desert land than with a quarrelsome and fretful woman."

This is the second verse I have used that describes how terrible it is for a man to have a quarrelsome wife. I did some research and found that the man God used to write these verses knew what he was talking about (and was spirit led). Solomon wrote these verses and he had many, many wives according to the Bible, a Harem, actually, so he knew a thing or two about quarrelsome women. How do you think your husband feels about living with you? He's not going to hear your answer, so go ahead, be honest with yourself. Are you a peaceful woman? Do you always have to get your way? Are you understanding? Helpful? Kind? Quarrelsome? Fretful? Make a conscious choice to make your home a fight-free zone. The Bible says as far as it depends on you then keep the peace. No, you can't control your husband's quarrelsomeness (yes, men can be quarrelsome too), but you can control you. Your husband will enjoy being home more when it is not a war zone and you can help create a better place for both of you to be. Fight for each other, not against one another!

Prayer:

Lord, help me to control my temper and help me to not be a fretful or quarrelsome wife. I pray my husband sees our home as a place of peace and safety. In Jesus's name, amen.

70

The Undoing of Self

2 Corinthians 13:5 (NIV) "Examine yourselves to see whether you are in the faith; test yourselves. Do you not realize that Christ Jesus is in you--unless, of course, you fail the test?"

For this devotion, I am going to ask you to strip yourself of all preconceived notions and who you think you are as a wife and really examine yourself with the Word of God. Not everything falls on you in marriage, but take a look at what does, and examine your ways as a wife. Have you been operating in faith? Is there anything hindering your progress of growth in God? Can you do more than what you're doing now to make your marriage better? The Bible says to test ourselves to see where we are at in the faith. Your salvation may never be in question, but the way you think may not be that of faith. Become undone before the Lord, showing Him every weak place, so that in your weakness, He is strong on your behalf. Self-examination should be a daily part of your routine. Whether it be in the morning when you wake up, with a cup of coffee in your hand, or at night, when you lay your head down on your pillow, make time to examine where you are in the faith. Your faith matters in marriage.

Prayer:

Lord, build my faith in You. Every day help me make the time to examine myself and my walk with You so that I may be better in all areas of my life, including as a wife. In Jesus's name, amen.

71

To Have and to Hold

Colossians 1:17 (NIV) "He is before all things, and in him all things hold together."

I know that you already know this and I hammered it home a couple of times, or three, or four, but invite God into your marriage in a bigger way than you ever have before. Did you know that God cares about every part of your relationship with your hubby? Before you and your husband ever said "I do," before you were ever born, before your husband was ever born, God knew you. He knew you! He knew your husband! He knows your marriage! The Bible says He knit you together; that means He knows what will sustain you. He knows what will keep you. God was before you were married, He is now, and He will always be . . . HE HOLDS ALL THINGS TOGETHER. Now, tell me again why He would not be able to hold your marriage together? God gave you that man to have and to hold. Invite God into your marriage again, afresh. Give Him reign over your spouse, marriage, and life. God is big enough to hold it all together if you place it in His hands.

Prayer:

Lord, I invite You into my marriage in a brand new way. I give You free reign over my feelings and my relationship with my husband to do what You see fit within my marriage, because I know You hold us together. In Jesus's name, amen.

72

Commit

Proverbs 16:3 (ESV) "Commit your work to the Lord, and your plans will be established."

Synonyms for commit would be pledge, devote, apply, dedicate . . . Sounds like marriage, right? You pledge yourself to your spouse and devote your time to them, applying love and effort, dedicating yourself one to the other. We live in a day and age where commitment is feared and strayed from when commitment is one of the greatest gifts we could give and/or receive. People want the next best thing when the original best thing is right in front of them. Your commitment level within marriage is a choice, *your choice*. You choose just how much of yourself you are willing to commit to your husband. Most likely, your husband would like to share every part of life with you, committing all to one another. Work on your dedication to your spouse and do what you can, where you can, to show him that you are committed and in it for the long haul. Marriage is not a race. It isn't even a marathon; it's more than that. It's a sacred union that you should hold on to dearly. Pledge yourself to a committed, godly relationship with your husband, one that will stand the test of time. The real fairy tale is growing old together.

Prayer:

Lord, I commit myself first to You and second to my
husband. I pray that we draw closer together,
dedicating and recommitting ourselves to one another.
In Jesus's name, amen.

73

One Hundred Percent

Colossians 3:23 (KJV) "And whatsoever ye do, do it heartily, as to the Lord, and not unto men."

Did you know that being a godly wife should be done as unto the Lord and not unto man? Give marriage your all. Give at 100 percent. Marriage was never meant for 50/50; it was meant for 100/100. You should give it 100 percent and your husband should give it 100 percent. The Word says that WHATEVER you do, it should be done heartily, which means sincerely, genuinely, profoundly. Be genuine with your spouse, with sincere affection and profound love. Your 100 percent does not have to look like anyone else's, just yours! As long as you are giving it your all and doing it as unto the Lord, that is what matters. Add God, remove selfishness, and marriage becomes pure, whole, and beautiful! Give your marriage 100 percent; it deserves your effort, time, and attention! I know a lot of times when I get home, I'm exhausted and I just give my husband the "leftover" energy I have, but God corrected me. I should give my husband the best of me. When you are at home don't just give your husband the rest of you, give him the BEST of you. Your marriage deserves the best!

Prayer:

Lord, not only do I want to give You 100 percent but I want to give my marriage 100 percent too. Let me work at my marriage as unto You and not unto man. In Jesus's name, amen.

74

A Kind Wife

Proverbs 11:16 (NIV) "A kindhearted woman gains respect, but ruthless men gain only wealth."

Have you ever wished for more respect in your relationship with your husband? According to the Word of God, a woman who is kindhearted *gains* respect. That means that through your kindhearted actions in your marriage, you can actually gain your husband's respect if he has not been so forthcoming with it to begin with. Yes, husbands should respect their wives no matter what, but what if you could gain even more respect through your words and actions? I can never get enough respect. I am pretty old-fashioned with my kids and have taught them yes ma'am, no ma'am, thank you, and please, because I have found this verse to be true. Kindness is kind of like a defensive weapon as it disarms people. If your husband is all up-in-arms (see what I did there), then show him a bit of kindness and see where it gets you. It may just get you the respect you have been looking for and it may just disarm his anger and diffuse the whole situation. It's important to see kindness not as a weakness, but as obedience to God and His Word. You are no one's doormat, but you could probably afford to be even kinder to your hubby, and in return, see the respect the Bible says kind women gain.

Prayer:

Lord, help me to be kind and gain my husband's respect. Teach me the difference between being too headstrong and set-in-my-ways and being a kind, yet still strong woman. In Jesus's name, amen.

75

Rest

Psalm 4:8 (ESV) "In peace I will both lie down and sleep; for you alone, O Lord, make me dwell in safety."

This word brings a smile to my face. *Rest.* In a society that says, "Go, go, go . . ." it's nice to know that God gives rest and actually made the human body require it. Rest is not a waste of time. There is a difference between rest and laziness. Working hard all day and wanting to go home to enjoy some nice peace and quiet is not being lazy, it's called rest. You should try it. You probably overexert yourself on a regular basis as a wife/mother. Take a moment to recover. Take a moment to rest. God is able to give you supernatural rest not only in your body, but in your mind too, where, let's be honest, most women need rest. If you have a lot going on and you're just overwhelmed in marriage or in life, take a deep breath, and ask God to give you rest. Rest from the burdens, rest from the bills, rest from the "hecticness" of life. Slow down. Sometimes you just need to take it easy and take care of yourself. Everything is going to be okay. The Bible says that when you lay down your head that your sleep will be sweet. Tonight, when you lie down, dwell in God's safety and let Him give you the rest you have been needing for so long. Your heart will be restless until you learn how to rest in God, for He is your resting place. Learn to find rest in Him!

Prayer:

Lord, give me rest. Rest in my body, mind, and soul. Remind me that it is okay to rest and that supernatural rest is found in You. In Jesus's name, amen.

76

The Misconception of Perfection

James 1:4 (ESV) "And let steadfastness have its full effect, that you may be perfect and complete, lacking in nothing."

Stepford wives . . . Do they even exist? No, because perfection is not real unless you are referring to Jesus Christ. The thing about perfection, outside of Jesus Christ, is that it is an illusion. Not even the most beautiful couple on earth is perfect. That's why you see stunning Hollywood couples get married only to get divorced a few years later. We all have our issues. It's not about how good we look on the outside that will keep us together. No, our perfection is not found in ourselves at all, but in Christ and Him alone. It's what is going on inside of you that resembles perfection in Christ. Part of what brings perfection in Christ is steadfastness. When we are steadfast in Christ, He can work in us continually, making us complete, and wanting nothing. What you nurture will grow, what you ignore will wither. Be steadfast in nurturing your marriage and remember, no one is perfect, so give grace and make room for your husband to grow. You know how you write a book? One word at a time. You know how you make a great marriage? Take one day at a time. I learned that once I quit chasing perfection and started following Christ, who is my perfection, my marriage grew stronger. Perfection belongs to God, let Him be your perfection.

Prayer:

Lord, help me to nurture my marriage and take care of my relationship with my husband. Allow me to remain steadfast, without wavering, and to depend on You for my perfection because I know it is You who makes me complete. In Jesus's name, amen.

77

The Original Couple

Psalm 139:14 (NIV) "I praise you because I am fearfully and wonderfully made; your works are wonderful, I know that full well."

You and your husband were both created unique; put you both together and you form a unique couple, one that cannot be duplicated. Not only are you both unique, but you both are fearfully and wonderfully made, which makes you an even more dynamic duo. Value your marriage as an original and you won't have to duplicate anyone else's. No two couples are the same. What works for one marriage may not work for the other (unless we are talking scripture and then it works for every couple, no questions asked). But I am talking about dinner routines, paying bills, vacations . . . those are all unique to individual couples. Embrace what makes your marriage *your* marriage! There are no other couples out there quite like you and your spouse. You and your husband are original, no need for imitations! God created you both to be original, so be original together!

Prayer:

Lord, make me appreciate the couple that my husband and I are. I know that we are both fearfully and wonderfully made and I want to embrace our uniqueness together. In Jesus's name, amen.

78

Unsatisfied to Satisfied

Proverbs 5:19 (KJV) "Let her be as the loving hind and pleasant roe; let her breasts satisfy thee at all times; and be thou ravished always with her love."

I did tell you that Solomon wrote most of Proverbs and he had many wives, right? Sometimes we like to skip over verses like these because we are bashful about such topics. I know I am. Yet, the Bible is full of verses that express love as physical too. What you do in your bedroom is between you and your husband, it is no one else's business. But if you're unsatisfied in marriage, I want you to go to the Word of God and read Song of Solomon. Read it as a guide to physical love between husband and wife. Believe it or not, you can go from unsatisfied in your marriage to satisfied with God's help. Yeah, God can even help your marriage right down to the physical love you receive from your husband. Do you remember when you first fell in love with him and were so attracted to him? You can get that back! Open the line of communication with your husband concerning physical love. Hold hands again. Kiss again. Fall in love all over again. Marriage can be both emotionally and physically satisfying when you follow God's plan for it! Plus, keeping friendship in mind, your marriage isn't solely physical. It's so much more. In marriage you come together and become one with your spouse in more than just the obvious way. Be satisfied in sharing hopes, dreams, and a future too!

Prayer:

Lord, help me to be satisfied in my marriage and help me to communicate to my husband what I need when it comes to physical and emotional love. In Jesus's name, amen.

79

God Is Able

2 Corinthians 9:8 (NIV) "And God is able to bless you abundantly, so that in all things at all times, having all that you need, you will abound in every good work."

ALL . . . Did you see how many times God reassures us that He is able to do ALL that we need, which includes helping you in your marriage? God is able to bless your relationship with your husband. He is able to bring you closer together. He is able to help both of you weather the storms together. God is able in all things at all times! What is it that you need in your marriage? What is it that you want in your marriage? God is able. Next time you have a doubt or have a need involving your relationship with your husband, I want you to say, "GOD IS ABLE!" Shout it if you have to. Just get it in your soul, get it in your mind that God can do what you need Him to do. He is a big God who cares about you and your marriage. Talk to Him about it. Go to God with your concerns. He is able to do exceedingly, abundantly, above all that you could even ask or think!

Prayer:

Lord, I know that You are able. I give You every part of me and my marriage because I know You can do more for my husband than I could ever imagine. You are good! You are able! In Jesus's name, amen.

80

Trust Fall

Acts 27:25 (NIV) "So keep up your courage, men, for I have faith in God that it will happen just as he told me."

Did you ever play the game "trust fall" when you were little, where you would stand with your back facing someone and trust them to catch you? Marriage is a lot like that. When you say "I do," you are placing your trust in someone and they are placing their trust in you. Marriage is a partnership of trust. The good thing about being a Christian wife is that you know someone who both you and your husband can trust, completely. You know that God's Word is true and that His promises for you are yea and amen. You know as you follow Christ, you will never be lost. It's the ultimate trust fall because you don't have to see God to know that He is there, and will catch you. He is there in your marriage and in your life. He is with you on the mountain top and He is with you in the valley. Keep up your courage and know that the Word of God does not return void. If He gave you a promise, that promise is going to happen just as He said it would.

Prayer:

Lord, I pray that I am putting all my trust in You. I trust
You with every part of my life, marriage included. The
promises You gave to me and my husband will come to
pass just as You said they would; let me never lose faith
or trust in You. In Jesus's name, amen.

81

Health & Wholeness

3 John 1:2 (NIV) "Dear friend, I pray that you may enjoy good health and that all may go well with you, even as your soul is getting along well."

I love how God allowed prayers from dear friends to be shown in the Bible. It teaches me how God would have me to pray for those that I love and cherish. In this passage, this letter is clearly written to encourage the recipient, stating well wishes for both physical and spiritual health. One prayer you should always have for your husband is that of health and wholeness. Encourage your husband and aim to lead him to a happy and healthy life. Most men would say that they do not want their wives nagging them about what they eat or their physical health, but if you show them that you care for their well-being, they might just start caring too. Together, you and your husband can work on being healthy and whole both physically and spiritually. Take one step at a time and ask God what each step should be to get you and your hubby to a place where both of you are healthy and whole.

Prayer:

Lord, I pray for both my and my husband's health. Help both of us become whole in mind, body, and spirit and show us the steps to take to become healthy in You. In Jesus's name, amen.

82

Looking to the Future

Jeremiah 29:11 (NIV) "For I know the plans I have for you, declares the LORD, plans to prosper you and not to harm you, plans to give you hope and a future."

God has a plan for you, God has a plan for your husband, and God has a plan for both of you together. In marriage, we can forget that God does indeed have a plan for us individually, and as a couple. God knew you and your husband before the beginning of time and saw fit to write a plan for your lives. Now, whether or not you and your husband follow His plan is entirely up to you and him. Each day you follow God is another step closer to you walking in His good plan for your life. There is a future God sees for you and your marriage, and it is one that is good, not evil, plans that offer hope and a future. In marriage, allow God to open the doors. He knows which ones you and your husband need to walk through. Look to the future by keeping your eyes on God! He has a great future for you and your marriage!

Prayer:

Lord, I know You have good plans for me, my husband, and my marriage. I pray that I follow those plans and keep my eyes on You. Help me and my husband know what doors to walk through in life. In Jesus's name, amen.

83

Affirmation

1 Thessalonians 5:11 (NIV) "Therefore encourage one another and build each other up, just as in fact you are doing."

Your husband needs your affirmation more than you likely know. An encouraging word from you just might have the power to change the course of his entire day, because when you speak words of affirmation to him they mean something to him, because you mean something to him. Yeah, some men are tough and macho, but I bet they love hearing their wife's adoration for them. Who doesn't like words of affirmation? Encourage your spouse before work, or when he gets home. Your words have the power of life and death . . . the Word says the tongue has the power of life or death. What is your tongue speaking? Your words matter. Start speaking words of affirmation to your husband. Good go-to phrases are: I appreciate you; I value what you do; I love you. Those simple phrases can bless your husband's soul when they come from your lips.

Prayer:

Lord, I give my tongue to You to use so that I may bring words of affirmation to my husband. Teach me the words he needs to hear that will encourage and inspire him. In Jesus's name, amen.

84

Depending on God

Psalm 62:7 (NIV) "My salvation and my honor depend on God; he is my mighty rock, my refuge."

It's important that you know and understand that your salvation does not depend on your husband, but on God. Depend on God for everything you need and you will never be disappointed. Husbands are human too, so they can't give us what we truly need; only God can. God is your rock within your marriage. He is your refuge. It's nice to have a supportive husband who is like a rock to you, but ultimately your strength is found in God and not anyone or anything else. Too often, we put a strain on our relationship with our spouses, expecting them to give us everything we need. Your husband can't fill the God-shaped hole in your heart. You must learn to depend on God for your every need because He is the cup from which you will drink and never thirst again. Don't put unnecessary pressures on your marriage because your husband is not filling something in you; depend on God to fill that place, for only He can.

Prayer:

Lord, I want to depend on You for everything I need. I know that only You can fill the void within me. You are my rock and You are my refuge. Teach me how to not put pressure on my husband that never belonged on him in the first place. In Jesus's name, amen.

85

Perfect Timing

Psalm 102:13 (NIV) "You will arise and have compassion on Zion, for it is time to show favor to her; the appointed time has come."

One of the hardest things to do is wait. We live in a fast-paced world, where everything is quick, made for convenience, and disposed of instead of repaired. In marriage there will be seasons of waiting—waiting to get pregnant, waiting to sell a house, waiting for that job promotion, etc. And it's not always convenient. In the season of waiting it is easy to give up, but if you hold on and wait on God, you will see the blessing come in His timing, which is the perfect time. God has a better vantage point and knows exactly what you need, and when you need it, plus where you need it. He is never late! The appointed time is coming, just wait and see the salvation of the Lord. Be still, and know that He is God! Next time you find yourself in the waiting room of life, remember who holds time in His hands. The blessing is on its way and will come in God's perfect timing! Hang in there, God's promises are on the way!

Prayer:

Lord, I know You hold time in Your hands and I pray that I wait on You and Your timing. Help me to stand still and see Your salvation. In Jesus's name, amen.

86

Frustration with Husband

Galatians 6:9 (ESV) "And let us not grow weary of doing good, for in due season we will reap, if we do not give up."

What can I say other than don't give up? Yes, there will be days where your husband frustrates the fire out of you. You just might frustrate the fire out of him too. Husbands have quirks about them that sometimes are not so endearing. The only thing you can do is communicate with him in a loving manner concerning what frustrates you. (Only if he can do something about it!!!) If it is not a simple fix then ask God to help your heart to not be so frustrated by it, or ask God to make the issue go away. The last thing you want to do is hurt your husband because you are simply, or not so simply, annoyed. Frustration happens, but what you do about it and how you handle it can change everything for the better. Example: So your husband clips his toenails in bed and it grosses you out? Kindly ask him to do it elsewhere without being rude about it. If he obliges, count it as a win! If he doesn't then pray and excuse yourself until he is done if you have to. I know that might not be what you want to hear, but my encouragement to you is don't be weary in doing good to your spouse. Never stop saying "I do"! You got this!

Prayer:

Lord, whatever frustrates me about my husband, I pray that You help me to deal with it in a loving manner. Let me not get weary in doing good to my husband and give me the strength to not give up! In Jesus's name, amen.

87

Laughing Together

Proverbs 17:22 (NIV) "A cheerful heart is good medicine, but a crushed spirit dries up the bones."

When was the last time you had a good laugh with your husband, where you weren't laughing at him, but with him? I'm talking that eye-watering type of laughter, where you throw your head back and don't even care what you look like. Maybe you are not the laughing couple type, but cheerful hearts are good for everyone; they're good for your marriage. A cheerful heart in marriage is as a medicine to your marriage. There is nothing quite like being with the ones you love and laughing. Scientifically, smiling, laughing, and just choosing to be happy releases endorphins, which are the body's natural "feel good" hormones. Next time you sit down with your husband, really enjoy him and who God has made him. Look into his eyes, engage, and commune with him. If you're the laughing type then laugh with him and enjoy his laughter as he enjoys yours. If not, at least be cheerful, like you appreciate his presence. You and your marriage deserve the best, and a cheerful heart will help get you there. Strengthen the marriage bones by laughing together!

Prayer:

Lord, make my heart cheerful and let me enjoy my husband. Let us enjoy each other. Help us to laugh together and talk together and be happy with one another. In Jesus's name, amen.

88

The Stress Factor

Matthew 11:29-30 (NIV) "Take my yoke upon you and learn from me, for I am gentle and humble in heart, and you will find rest for your souls. For my yoke is easy and my burden is light."

Sometimes we have those days that are just unbearable, the days where we could swear that we were gaining gray hairs by the minute. As a wife and as a mother, there is no shortage of stress. It can be found at every turn. I know you may have a lot on your plate and you're going all the time, running around trying to do everything that has to get done and it's stressful. God knew that this life was going to be burdensome and full of stress, so He offers us another option. He tells us to take upon His yoke, for his burden is light. You see, God traded us. For our heavy-laden hearts, He offers gentleness and rest for our weary souls. Right where you are, give God your stress, no matter what's causing it. He can take it and He can give you relief. Doesn't it feel better to let go and let God? Inhale . . . Exhale . . . Find your relief by taking every stress factor upon your shoulders and then give it to God. A practical way to relieve stress is to find out what can wait and what cannot, what needs to be taken care of today and what can wait for tomorrow. You are super woman, yes, but you are still only one woman. Give God your stress.

Prayer:

Lord, I relinquish all of my stress to You. Thank You for giving me Your yoke which is easy and Your burden which is light. Thank You for trading me! Give me wisdom on what I need to do now and what can wait. In Jesus's name, amen.

89

The Understanding Wife

Proverbs 19:14 (NLT) "Fathers can give their sons an inheritance of houses and wealth, but only the LORD can give an understanding wife."

Are you an understanding wife? Let's take a closer look at what understanding really means in marriage. It means to be sympathetically aware of your husband's feelings. It means to be tolerant of him. It means to have insight and good judgment when it comes to him. Are you those things? I must admit that I still need some work on understanding my husband, because sometimes, I just don't. Understanding your husband is a process and takes time. An understanding wife is from God, so make sure you go to God when you are trying to understand and be understanding toward your husband. Be sympathetically aware of his needs, tolerant of his hobbies (to an extent, I know), and do your best to understand where he is coming from. Example of The Understanding Wife: Learning what buttons he hates having pushed and then not pushing them is a great start!

Prayer:

Lord, I pray that I am an understanding wife. Help me to be sympathetically aware and learn my husband better so that I may know how to be a better wife to him. In Jesus's name, amen.

90

Comfort Zone

2 Corinthians 1:4 (NIV) ". . . who comforts us in all our troubles, so that we can comfort those in any trouble with the comfort we ourselves receive from God."

Having a comfort zone is not always a bad thing, especially when it comes to marriage. In fact, our husbands should feel comfortable with us. They should feel free with us and safe. God says that He is our comfort through our troubles and that we can give that same comfort to others, and should. Be a shoulder to cry on for your husband, be a hand to hold, be a listening ear, *just be there.* By being there you provide a source of comfort for your husband that no one else can provide. You know him intimately, you know his fears, and his dreams. You are the person he wants to be there for him in his time of trouble. As God is there for both you and your husband, let your marriage be a place of comfort, where one can run to the other. This is a comfort zone that you don't have to force yourself out of, but rather, is a good place to go in your marriage. Comfort your husband as God comforts you.

Prayer:

Lord, I want to be a comfort zone for my husband. Let my husband know he can count on me to be a giver of comfort when he needs it and as You comfort me, give me the strength to comfort others. In Jesus's name, amen.

91

Life Support

Romans 12:12 (NIV) "Be joyful in hope, patient in affliction, faithful in prayer."

Life support keeps the body alive by doing the work the body would normally do, so what do you do when it seems like your marriage is on life support? You fight. Just like your body would fight to stay alive. But you don't fight like other wives have to fight; you fight with God by your side. You know to fight on your knees through prayer. You know to praise. You know to worship. If I strive to save my marriage on my own, I strive in vain. I cannot do it on my own. I need someone stronger, greater, and bigger than I am. I need God. God tells us, in life, to be joyful in hope, patient in affliction, and faithful in prayer. As wives, we need to apply this to our marriages, especially when we feel like they . . . *we* . . . may be falling apart. God can save your marriage and breathe life into it again. The longer you're married, the more opportunities for conflict, but through it all, God is greater. Don't pull the plug on your marriage until you have sought God. You may just find that it was a lull/slump or a speedbump, a growing pain, if you will. Miracles happen and God can bring marriages back to life!

Prayer:

Lord, if there is ever a time where I feel like my marriage is on life support, walk me through it, and remind me You are there to help me through it. Breathe life into my marriage and into me as a wife. In Jesus's name, amen.

92

Bond of Peace

Ephesians 4:2-3 (NIV) "Be completely humble and gentle; be patient, bearing with one another in love. Make every effort to keep the unity of the Spirit through the bond of peace."

As wives, we are to be humble—not prideful or arrogant—and be gentle, patient, bearing with our husbands in love. Pride has no place in marriage. It is our job not only as wives, but as Christians, to make every effort to keep the unity of the Spirit through the bond of peace. Are you making the effort? With your husband, there should be a bond of peace that both of you can count on. If you are married to a man who is not peaceful, pray for him and do everything on your part to bring about peace in your home. The bond of peace will strengthen your marriage and your love. Peace in the dictionary is described as the non-warring condition of a nation. As far as it depends on you, can you make your home a non-warring nation? The love in your marriage should not be a battlefield. God can help your marriage and make it a better place to live. Be a part of the bond of peace!

Prayer:

Lord, I want to be a wife of peace, a wife who is humble, gentle, and patient. Allow me to bear with my husband in love. In Jesus's name, amen.

93

Relinquishing Anger

Ephesians 4:31 (NIV) "Get rid of all bitterness, rage and anger, brawling and slander, along with every form of malice."

In the previous devotion, we covered peace, but what do we do when we are angry? Anger is a natural human emotion and, most likely, as wives, we will experience it in our relationship at one time or the other. The Bible clearly says to get rid of it. The Bible also says to not sin in your anger (Ephesians 4:26). While anger is a natural emotion, it gives access to sin through rage, bitterness, and malice. Even if we are angry, it does not give us an excuse to sin. The only way we can get rid of anger is to relinquish it to God. To do that, we must give God whatever has made us so angry and go to the Lord in prayer, seek His Word, and praise Him. Praising God and giving Him thanks brings God into the situation. He can help bring you down off an "anger ledge." It's hard to remain angry when you're giving the God who created you praise and thanksgiving. You do not have to blow up. There are better ways to handle your anger and God will help you do so. If you struggle with anger, seek God, and make note of your "triggers." When you feel like you are about to lose control with your spouse, slow down, take a moment, and count to ten, ask God for help, and then respond.

Prayer:

Lord, I relinquish every last drop of rage to You. I don't want to be bitter, brawling, or slanderous. Help me to overcome anger in a godly way. In Jesus's name, amen.

94

The Right Track

Isaiah 26:7 (NIV) "The path of the righteous is level; you, the Upright One, make the way of the righteous smooth."

What is the right track in your marriage? Take the righteous way! To be righteous is to be morally and Biblically right and justified. When you do what the Word says and follow God's command, He considers you righteous, and that's a place where you want to be found. When you are righteous in your marriage, obeying God's commands, He makes your path level and smooth. Of course, there are a few bumps and rocks in marriage, because we have all fallen short of His glory, but when we get back up, dust ourselves off, and seek His face, He puts us on the right track again. Look at your marriage and ask if you are on the right track with your husband. Are there bumps in the road? What can you do about them? What does the Word say? It's crucial you know the Word of God for yourself so that no matter what may come your way, you have a verse to stand on and pray. God will set you on the right track in your marriage when you obey what He has said. Become the righteous woman of God that He has called you to be and let God place your marriage on the right track!

Lord, place my husband and me on the right track for our marriage. Help us both to follow You and Your commands concerning marriage, and life. In Jesus's name, amen.

95

Speak Life into your Marriage

Ezekiel 37:1-5 (ESV) "The hand of the Lord was upon me, and he brought me out in the Spirit of the Lord and set me down in the middle of the valley; it was full of bones. And he led me around among them, and behold, there were very many on the surface of the valley, and behold, they were very dry. And he said to me, 'Son of man, can these bones live?' And I answered, 'O Lord God, you know.' Then he said to me, 'Prophesy over these bones, and say to them, O dry bones, hear the word of the Lord. Thus says the Lord God to these bones: Behold, I will cause breath to enter you, and you shall live.'"

While I was speaking to the ladies at my church one night, I said something that made me really reflect upon what I thought and said about my own marriage. I said, "My marriage shall live and not die." I said that after referring to how many marriages were failing. I can see the devil attacking the sanctity of marriage by making divorce so rampant, even in the church. In the verse above, we see God telling his servant to speak to the dry bones and He would make them live. There may be times when things are hard in your marriage, but I challenge you to speak life into your marriage. Watch how you think about your husband, and be careful what you say about him. Never slander your husband when talking to family or friends. Speak life. Think of the positive within marriage and get rid of the negative thoughts you may have had about your husband. What you say and think seep in to how you feel and behave. I pray the hand of the Lord is upon you and that you speak to the dry bones in your marriage and say, "My marriage shall live and not die!"

Prayer:

Lord, be upon me and guide me in my marriage. Help me to guard what I say and think about my husband and remove any negative feelings that may have attached themselves to my heart over the years. My marriage shall live and not die! In Jesus's name, amen.

96

Thankfulness for Husband

Ephesians 5:20 (NIV) ". . . always giving thanks to God the Father for everything, in the name of our Lord Jesus Christ."

Your husband is awesome! I mean, I am just guessing he is because you chose him and he chose you, which also makes him really smart because you are a great catch! When was the last time you thanked God for your husband's awesomeness? My husband always jokingly says, "Do you ever just wake up in the morning and thank God for how awesome I am?" This is usually after he has done something really nice for me and he's totally joking, but I *should* thank God for him. I am grateful for him and everything he does. There's got to be at least one thing your husband does that you are grateful for and probably tons more! Go on, and thank God for him! You know what else would really be nice? Telling your husband "thank you." Thank you for being here. Thank you for getting the oil changed in my car. Thank you for treating me to dinner. Thank you for working so hard. Thank you for loving me like you do. What can you tell your husband "thank you" for? It can be something really small or really big, but say it and say it often.

Prayer:

Lord, make me grateful for my husband. I am thankful for his awesomeness. Thank You, God, for blessing me with a husband. Help me to say, "Thank you," to him more often. In Jesus's name, amen.

97

Importance of Discernment

Proverbs 17:24 (NIV) "A discerning person keeps wisdom in view, but a fool's eyes wander to the ends of the earth."

Never let your eyes wander down the road of greener pastures. Water your marriage and watch it be replenished. Keep wisdom in your relationship with your husband and discern his moods and when the right time would be to bring something up. God will give you discernment to tell when is the right time to speak with your husband about certain things and, when you take heed to God's direction, He will give you favor with your husband. Use wisdom when approaching your husband, especially when it comes to sensitive topics. The importance of discernment in marriage is for the benefit of both the wife and husband. A discerning wife knows just how to operate her household, and how and when to speak to her husband regarding certain matters. She is quick to listen and slow to speak, which is a highly valued trait in anyone. God can use a discerning wife and discernment will give her access to her husband's heart in a way that she would not normally have. Learn to discern!

Prayer:

Lord, give me discernment and wisdom. Let me hold them close in my marriage. Help me to grasp when the timing is right to bring up certain things and then let me say them the way You would want me to. In Jesus's name, amen.

98

Expressions of Love

1 John 4:7 (ESV) "Beloved, let us love one another, for love is from God, and whoever loves has been born of God and knows God."

Ah, here we are again on the topic that really starts all marriages . . .*love.* There are many different expressions of love and most are not these big, grand gestures. One spouse may feel love through words, the other through actions. Whatever the case may be, be sure to give your husband the type of love that he craves. If your husband feels loved through touch, then brush your hand along his back as you walk by and give him a smile. If he prefers words, then tell him how much you love him. If he prefers acts of service, then pick up his dry cleaning for him and surprise him. There are never-ending ways you can show your spouse love. Express your love for your spouse and tune in to what he likes and how he feels loved. And if he is not loving you in your love language, then talk to him and let him know how you want to be loved too. Relationship is a partnership after all, where both parties give of themselves to show the other love. Speak your husband's love language!

Prayer:

Lord, I pray that I express my love to my husband in a way that he understands. Show me how he likes to receive love so that I may give him the love he craves from me. I also pray for him to love me in the way that I crave too, and through this process let us both love more. In Jesus's name, amen.

99

Heartfelt

Ezekiel 36:26 (ESV) "And I will give you a new heart, and a new spirit I will put within you. And I will remove the heart of stone from your flesh and give you a heart of flesh."

Have you ever heard the phrase, "She's as cold as ice"? It's a song, right? Anyway, I have never heard of a cold-hearted woman being a good thing and "ice cold," yeah, I don't really think it's a term of endearment. Has your heart grown cold? Do you have a hard heart in any area of your life? If so, this could spill over into your marriage. Many of the issues we deal with in marriage, and in life, are heart issues. God says that He will give us a new heart. He will remove the heart of stone and give us a heart of flesh so that we may know Him. Do a heart check right now. Any hard places? Any places that are cold against your husband? Give God the scalpel and let Him operate. God can operate on your heart through the Word, so stay in it and keep growing, and allow God to bring warmth into your heart. Give yourself permission to feel again, care again, and love again in a heartfelt way!

Prayer:

Lord, take away any places in my heart that are stony and replace it with a heart of flesh that feels You and knows You. If there are any areas in my heart that are hardened against my husband, even if I don't see them, chip them away, and make my heart new. In Jesus's name, amen.

100

Time to Praise

Psalm 147:1-5 (ESV) "Praise the Lord! For it is good to sing praises to our God; for it is pleasant, and a song of praise is fitting. The Lord builds up Jerusalem; he gathers the outcasts of Israel. He heals the brokenhearted and binds up their wounds. He determines the number of the stars; he gives to all of them their names. Great is our Lord, and abundant in power; his understanding is beyond measure."

Here we are at devotion one hundred. For the final stamp of God's approval, let's put a praise on it! Just as the scripture says, I do think a song of praise is fitting. You have come a long way and I hope you have been encouraged, and maybe even challenged. God is gathering His people. Christian wives, you are part of His plan, and His plans are always good. Keep striving in your marriage. Remember the Lord is abundant in power and His understanding is beyond measure. Acknowledge Him in your marriage and you will find Him in your marriage. Give God place in your relationship with your husband and God will be there. Give God praise for your marriage and for your husband. Not everyone makes it, but as for you and your husband, serve the Lord, and your marriage will not only survive, but thrive. I hope and pray that each of you reading this grow old with the husband of your youth and that one day you can look back at all you both have been through and say, "Baby, we made it!" May you and your husband be as happy as the elderly couples who still hold hands and look each other in the eyes with love, compassion, and devotion, because that's the real fairy tale.

Prayer:

Lord, I praise You for everything that You have done for me. I praise You for my marriage. I praise You for my husband. Knit us tightly together and let our love be the type of love that lasts. In Jesus's name, amen.

Dear Reader,

Thank you so much for taking the time to read *The Real Life of a Christian Wife*. I want you to know that I am rooting for your marriage; more importantly, God is rooting for your marriage. Please know that you are not alone. Being a Christian wife is no "cake walk." As I wrote this book, I cried, I prayed, and I thanked God for my own marriage, AND I saw the areas that I need to work on as a wife. God brought me closer to my own husband and made me a better wife through the process of writing this book, so even if it was just for me, it was worth it, but I really hope it's for you, too! I hope that your relationship with your husband is strengthened and that you are encouraged to be everything God said a wife could be. God's standards are different than the world's and I pray you see yourself through His lens. He has a much greater perspective! Your marriage belongs in God's hands and no one else's; be sure it stays in the right place. Praying for you, my fellow Christian wives! May we build each other up and not tear each other down. Praying for your spouses, too, that they be the men of God in a way that is befitting for a Christian wife to have—that they love you, cherish you, and appreciate you for all that you do.

Again, thank you for reading! My heart is full of gratitude!

If you enjoyed the prayers and devotions found in this book, would you mind helping to spread the word by leaving a review on Amazon? If you have the time, I'd be so blessed by it!

Blessings,

Mandy Fender

Connect

I would absolutely love to connect with you on social media!

Website:mandyfender.com

Facebook: Mandy Fender

Twitter: @mandyfender11

Instagram: Mandy.Fender

Goodreads: Mandy Fender

Made in the USA
Las Vegas, NV
24 November 2023

81423806R10125